County Council

Libraries, books and more.........

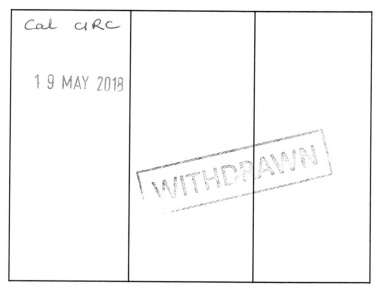
Please return/renew this item by the last date due.
Library items may also be renewed by phone on
030 33 33 1234 (24 hours) or via our website

www.cumbria.gov.uk/libraries

Cumbria Libraries

Interactive Catalogue

Ask for a CLIC password

Best After

Basic Instructions on Being a Human

Eini Neve

© 2016 Eini Neve
einineve.com
eini.neve@gmail.com

Available also in Finnish
Neve, Eini. 2015. Parasta jälkeen — Ihmisyyden perusoppimäärä.
Helsinki: Books on Demand GmbH.

Illustration and layout
Eini Neve

Proofreading
Robert Badeau, Aura Professional English Consulting
auraenglish.com

Publisher
BoD – Books on Demand GmbH, Helsinki, Finland

Producer
BoD – Books on Demand GmbH, Norderstedt, Germany

ISBN 978-952-330-375-1

Contents

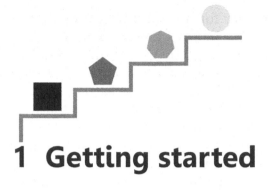

1 Getting started

You will be able to cast a foundation for proper human existence and maturation with these teachings. This book is like a sack of concrete, which gets its water from your reading. From that wet concrete, you will cast an even slab floor as a basis for your mental health and maturation into an authentic adult.

Some cast their foundation on solid ground, while some have a plot that is more challenging. Perhaps a soft or wet ground requires pilings or a steep cliff plot extraction. Challenging construction sites belong to at least those who are dispirited, depressed, easily irritable, constantly angry, guilt-ridden, inefficient, or perfectionists. They need to work slightly harder, and the first part of this book is particularly for them. On the other hand, everyone benefits simultaneously from these early teachings.

This kind of foundation casting theory ought to belong to every person's basic syllabus. Why? Because in roughly 40 percent of families, children get an upbringing, the damages of which are being solved late into their adulthood — if they even get solved. Stop and think about that number for a second. Don't you agree that 40 percent is a huge number? Almost in half of the families, children don't receive sufficient instructions for life. It seems mind-boggling that societies maintain such a blind spot and don't try to stand in for this limitation, for instance, during the children's compulsory education.

What price does mankind pay for the fact that nearly half of its people are missing the basic teachings of how to exist as a stable, contented, and mature human being? The price paid shows itself as bullying at homes, schools, workplaces, and on the internet. It manifests itself as mental health issues. It is visible from the early retirement numbers due to mental health reasons. Take for instance Finland, a small Nordic country with a population of less than 5.5 million, yet 16 people retire early every single day due to mental health reasons (Finnish Centre for Pensions; statistics 2012 and 2013). Early retirement figures due to mental health problems are similar in all the developed, Western countries. This a second point for you to consider. Aren't such rates alarming? These high level early retirement figures don't even include those who persevere all the way to the statutory retirement age despite their unhappiness and mental problems. These figures don't include those who never retire. With that I am referring especially to those who are victims of self-destruction. These all are some of the indications that nearly half of the people haven't built their houses — that is: themselves — on an even slab. It is hard to build when one doesn't know how to do it.

A negative, unhappy life attitude is widespread. If there was a common root behind such unhappiness, what would it be? I believe and will try to convince you while reading this book that at least one major cause for such unhappiness is deficiency in social maturation. Social maturation could also be called maturation into an authentic adult. Similar findings have been made before. For example, psychiatrist *M. Scott Peck* has earlier said something similar when he expressed that growth in mental health and growth in spirituality is one and the same thing. Spiritual growth and maturation into an authentic adult have, in fact, much in common. The main connecting factor is a highly developed ability to put oneself in another person's shoes. Perhaps spiritual growth and maturation into an authentic adult is also one and the same thing.

Imagine that maturation into an authentic adult is depicted with a long segment, along which one moves as he matures. Then let's put a negative, unhappy life attitude at the beginning end of that segment. From that segment end, we should drag ourselves towards the center, that is, towards healthier and happier regions. How is that done? First of all, we need to begin with the very basics. The very first basic item we need to focus on is *a thought*. Everything starts from refining our thoughts into a better shape. The next basic element is *a silent assumption*. Silent assumptions are our assumptions and beliefs about ourselves, other people, this life, and the world. Assumptions are therefore silent because they do not make much noise about their existence, but they show themselves, however, all the time in "everything"— in opinions, behaviors, and choices. Hence progression along the maturation segment requires also refining silent assumptions. We also need to develop our capacity for empathy, overcome our fallacy of control, and learn to carry the right amount of responsibility. This process is crowned with love, moderation, persistence, patience, and an order. At this point this all may sound a bit cryptic and maybe a bit laborious and even frightening, but everything will become clearer and easier as we move forward.

By sowing proper thoughts and actions, we eventually reap social maturity. Thus, we get a basic rule for mental health: the higher the social maturity level, the better the mental health. Just as well we could also say that the more authentic the adult, the better the mental health.

The starting end of the maturation segment inhabits also *feelings of worthlessness*. In case of a depressed person, those feelings may stem from this kind of thinking: "I never ever succeed in anything. I'm a total, worthless 'loser.' There's no point in trying." A low-spirited person may slander himself with slightly milder thoughts like "I have this flaw and that flaw. Then I have that flaw too."

What makes a person feel worthless and insecure? For the majority of people those damages arise from the lovelessness of a home or a growth milieu. This lovelessness may have been highlighted by chaos and a possible abandonment or simply by threats of abandonment. Chaos is unpredictability, immoderation, and lack of continuity and an order. Where does this lovelessness come from? There are the same factors in the background from which you yourself may suffer: distorted thought patterns, distorted or out-dated silent assumptions, and premature stagnation in maturation into an authentic adult.

Highly sensitive people may be more susceptible to depression under poor circumstances, but even then the main reason is the absence of love. The main ingredient in human maturation is, indeed, love. As long as the clearly recognizable undercurrent of love is always present, parents may be forgiven even for big mistakes in their child-rearing — and it's a law of nature that every human parent makes mistakes.

It is unfortunate that some of us have to start from the very extreme end of the social maturation segment, while others have the better fortune to start closer to the middle. The more fortunate ones are those who have always been loved and valued, and who have learned good thought patterns from the get-go.

Nonetheless social maturation is possible for everyone because we all are capable of making changes in our thinking. Distorted thought patterns go *always* hand in hand with mental disorders. Furthermore, thoughts *produce* brain chemistry, even though at first it is really hard to believe and accept that. Everybody can modify their thoughts, if they want to. Thus everybody is able to alter their own brain chemistry. Thus everybody is able to heal their own mental health.

Teachings from the classics, newer books, articles and videos from the field of mental health have been collected in this book. Major source material is located in the References section, but otherwise very little reference is made to the sources in order to keep your attention on the topic. Existing knowledge yielded also new knowledge. Among the new and previously unpublished are the new distorted thought pattern "families" and the fallacy of control in social immaturity. Finally, these new observations had a great impact in how the final jigsaw is formed. That is to say, how negativity, depression, anxiety disorders, personality disorders, a maturation into an authentic adult, positivity, happiness are linked intelligibly to one another.

In the beginning of each chapter there is a set of figures in which there is a square on the lowest level of a staircase and a circle on the highest. Those forms represent healing, development, and maturation of a human being. We start as a square and seek to become a circle. Flawless circles — perfectly well-balanced human beings — don't exist or at least there are so few of them that we don't need to burden our minds with that thought. All the more there are those of us who are angular at different degrees. Teachings collected in this book help to grind those corners and edges smoother.

There are many paths to the final step of almost becoming a circle. For instance, religion can be a route to some to a near circle, but it can also be a path that keeps a person in a square form. The very same thing can therefore act totally differently for different people and in turn one can reach a similar end result via different routes.

How is it possible that well-meaning religious or spiritual teachings of no particular creed can produce a square? There are probably many reasons for that. Abilities, maturity level, and silent assumptions of both a distributor and a recipient surely play a role. One reason worthwhile pointing out is also the fact that teachings often start from too far up. That is, quite often these teachings relate to building the first level or the attic. If the foundation has not yet been cast or it is askew or hollow, then well-meaning teachings intended to be noble, good, and promote positive thinking may evoke only annoyance and anger. If the foundation has not yet been cast or it is askew or hollow, an alternative may also be a superficial adoption of doctrines as a set of rules. This book starts from the basics how a person can *first* cast an even, solid foundation on to which it is safe and smart to build.

Teachings in the first part of this book are based on cognitive psychotherapy. A cognition is just a fancy word for a thought. Hence in cognitive psychotherapy, the focus is on thinking. Healing and maturation begin when a person observes his own thinking and silent assumptions, and insofar as he notices them distorted, he starts the straightening work. This is a very conscious action. A slogan for cognitive psychotherapy could then well be: Health through awareness!

Usually people have a false presumption that *feelings* automatically flood into their mind. However, the fact remains that you can't feel low-spiritedness, sadness, bubbling joy, perplexing love — nothing what so ever — before your brain processes first what is happening around you. Your brain processes first everything you experience and sense, such as: smelling, tasting, hearing, seeing or touching; and one of the end results is a feeling or feelings. First you have to understand on at least some level what is going on before you can have any feelings about it. If you get a positive understanding, your thoughts are positive and lead to positive feelings. If your impression is negative, you think negatively and you will have negative feelings. Neutral impressions and thoughts lead to neutral feelings. Only reflexes remain outside of this explanation. They only swing around the spinal cord and don't reach the brain.

Quite often people have also a false presumption that *thoughts* are born automatically. They claim they have to be automatic, because no one would think voluntarily negative thoughts and make themselves willfully miserable. The culprit is, however, a very firmly fixed habit in which case it only feels as if the thoughts form automatically. You may have some difficulty accepting this concept in the beginning, but you are in fact constantly at the controls. On the other hand, the fact that you are constantly at the controls is the hope-offering fact. You only need to steer better, and that is a skill that can be fully learned and mastered.

1.1 Change through reading?

First off you need to be infused with a trust that it is certainly possible to heal from low-spiritedness, depression, and several other negative feelings and habits only by reading. This kind of understanding and healing through reading is called reading therapy, that is, *bibliotherapy*. Bibliotherapy is approved and accepted in science. Scientific research on the effects of bibliotherapy has been done, for instance, on the book *Feeling good* by *David D. Burns*. Researchers were only surprised by the fact that the effects of bibliotherapy were even better after three years than right after completing reading. This surprising observation found finally its explanation: people who participated in this research sought repeatedly upliftment for their spirits from bibliotherapy when they were faced with adversity. This kind of repetition worked like a booster shot. Bibliotherapy, which is based on cognitive psychotherapy, is exactly this kind of "plowing of the thought field."

If you already know that you are depressed or you find it out when you do a depression test, for instance, on the internet, you may heal better through bibliotherapy. When bibliotherapy is compared to drug therapy, the outcome is *better* and *very long-lasting*. Statistically the difference in treatment success is significant.

Nonetheless some depressed people benefit from drug therapy or their healing even requires it. Sometimes drug therapy is also a good way to settle down a brain so it is able to receive therapy, which will put thoughts into new grooves. If you are currently in psychotherapy or receiving drug therapy, bibliotherapy may speed significantly your healing. In other words, different treatments are not conflicting, instead they support each other. This, too, is an outcome from a scientific study.

Drug therapy will not be dealt with in this book after this. You are only left with three reminders about medications:

1. Alcohol and drugs don't work as antidepressants. They worsen the mood further so there is an excellent reason to call them depressants. At the same time, they can be called stoppers of social maturation.
2. If your antidepressant doesn't seem to have an effect, it is not your fault. None of the practitioners are so omniscient that they can prescribe with certainty the right medication and the right dosage from the get-go. Recovery may require several experimentations.
3. Every single person on this planet needs continuous medication and that means eating proper and real food. Processed foods don't represent quality fuel.

Did that previous section produce a thought in your mind that you are a case that needs drug therapy, and there is no way you can heal simply by only reading this book? If you truly thought so, your *thoughts* produced *feelings*. Did those feelings include despair, cynicism, annoyance, or even hate? We move constructively forward if you replace that possible previous thought with a new thought: "This time I won't jump to conclusions right away. I will also restrain myself from making objections after every single sentence." If you said that new thought to yourself whole-heartedly, it produced at least a weak flicker of hope, that is, a feeling that will suffice perfectly well as a prime mover. With that flicker of hope, we will investigate next the truth about self-worth.

1.2 Self-worth and self-esteem

Self-worth and self-esteem are often used interchangeably. In this book it is seen that self-worth is the very core and self-esteem is more of an icing on top of it. You may feel that you have high self-esteem, that is, you know that you are quite good and competent and perhaps you are even very successful, but at the same time you may have a nagging feeling that you are not loveable and worthy. Such a nagging feeling exposes the core, low self-worth. You can never have genuinely high self-esteem if you feel you don't have high self-worth. Therefore, we will focus here on self-worth instead of self-esteem. Self-worth is often also referred to as dignity. Self-confidence is, in turn, a belief and trust that one succeeds in works and activities, which one is undertaking.

How does self-worth show itself in practice? It shows itself in thoughts, speech, humor, silent assumptions, choices, behavior, maturity, satisfaction, and happiness. Because it shows itself in choices, thereby it shows itself, among other things, in a choice of a career and a spouse or in a choice not to have one. It shows itself through general health, because it has an effect how good care one takes of oneself. It shows itself through mental health, for instance, in a depression or even whether or not a person develops a personality disorder. Hence it shows itself in everything.

Let's assume that two drivers aim to drive exactly the same distance in the exactly same horrible blizzard. One of them is very skillful and experienced in driving, but his self-worth is low. The other one is a mediocre driver, but his self-worth is high. Unexpectedly the ride of that skillful driver ends in a snowbank, whereas the mediocre driver arrives to the destination. The difference is that the mediocre driver drove with caution because he was carrying a valuable cargo. Thus self-worth shows itself even in an end result of a short drive. Therefore, self-worth should be the most important thing for you here and now.

If a person is unhappy, dispirited, depressed, easily irritable, constantly angry, guilt-ridden, inefficient, or a perfectionist, he *invariably* has low self-worth. Thus he feels worthless, loveless, and he has low respect towards himself.

The more severe the depression, the stronger a person believes in his worthlessness. According to research, 80 percent of depressed people feel even repulsion towards themselves. According to this same research, depressed people feel deficiency, for instance, in their intelligence, appearance, success, and popularity.

For starters, high self-worth is not based on these above-mentioned qualities. High self-worth is not even based on massive assets. Many loved, famous, talented, good-looking, and wealthy victims of self-destruction provide us evidence for that.

High self-worth is not built on acceptance and success, but low self-worth is. People with low self-worth observe themselves through the eyes of other people. They ponder constantly what other people may be thinking about them. The measuring stick they use for their self-worth is external achievements, material possessions, and quality of human contacts. In addition, people with low self-worth wear magnifying glasses as their eyeglasses. When they look at the world through those glasses, every insignificant mistake, imperfection, limitation, or deficiency gets magnified into an overwhelming failure.

Before we proceed to the real truth about self-worth, let's lighten the mood with this saying "You wouldn't worry so much about what others think of you, if you realized how seldom they do." *Eleanor*

Roosevelt is considered to be the mother of this saying. *Wayne Dyer*, in turn, has said "What other people think of me is none of my business."

You can't earn your self-worth from what you have accomplished. Accomplishments, significant contacts, and status symbols bring satisfaction, but they don't increase your genuine self-worth. The first bigger adversity brings crushingly down self-worth built on such external trappings and trimmings. An adversity is, indeed, a litmus test for the genuineness of one's self-worth.

The time has come for you to hear the truth about your self-worth. This truth is that your worth was determined already at that moment you were created, that worth is immeasurable, and that worth remains. You are in your full worth *always*. You may think that you are being imposed with some religious definition. On the contrary, this is a very rational, practical definition based on a free choice. Happy and well-balanced people have chosen exactly this definition. They are constantly in their full worth no matter what happens to them. They feel worthy even if they lose their jobs, experience bankruptcy, are abandoned, or get seriously ill.

Undoubtedly you have heard criticism during your lifetime. Perhaps criticism is even a mild statement in your case, if you have been a target of nastiness, shouting, slander, bullying, and denigration. Most probably you have heard something negative, if you're now dispirited or depressed and have low self-worth. You may have never thought about it, but you have the power to choose how you allow other people's criticism affect you. Because you have the power to choose how you react, in the end, only you yourself can pose a threat to your self-worth. Understandably you may resist this idea. You may say "You have not been there and listened to those constant malicious remarks like I have. I have listened to how I know nothing, I will never learn anything and how I am a total 'loser.' When you hear enough of it, there's no other option but to start believing in it."

It is wrong and sad if you have received that kind of treatment. Your mood will improve from this tremendously as soon as you learn a new way to receive criticism. When you used your old way, criticism made you either sad or angry. Once you adopt a new way, your mood stays more neutral, and you won't get as much of a dent in your self-worth.

Most of the people become sad from criticism. Perhaps this applies to you too. In case it does, then you automatically assume that your critic is absolutely right. Without much thought, you jump to a conclusion that, indeed, you were wrong or you did something wrong. If you are depressed, you magnify the importance of that criticism with your distorted thought patterns. For instance, you may think that you are a "loser." You may also think "A fumbler like this shouldn't try anything in the future." You may also magnify the importance of your mistake by thinking "once the word starts to spread, no one will ever employ me." With your distorted, negative thinking you lift your mistake on the podium and focus all the spotlights on it — and you feel depressed. Towards your critic, you may be passive, shiftless, and evasive. Quite possibly you withdraw from the situation.

Some people relate to criticism by getting angry. Even some of the depressed people choose this angry approach. Maybe this applies to you too? When you receive criticism, you immediately get defensive. You may heap accusations on your critic because you assume that the best defense is a fire-and-brimstone offense. At the same time, you persistently refuse to admit that you could have in any way done a mistake. If you admitted to it, at the same time, you would admit that you are a worthless person. For a short moment you may feel triumphant if you managed to slate your critic. In the long run the end result may be a rupture in your relationship. When that happens, then you may feel really unhappy.

There is yet another way to meet criticism. This third way is a good way because your mood remains calmer and more contented. This is a way that is already used by those with high self-worth. When you face criticism, decide first if that criticism is right or wrong. Because it is quite possible that that criticism is not justified. If your critic is wrong, there is no need for you to hurt your feelings. It is his mistake, not yours. If, instead, you realize that you made a mistake, you still don't need to feel sad or upset about it because we all make mistakes. You can't be expected to be perfect. No one needs to be perfect.

It is easy to admit having made a mistake when you don't mix the deed with the doer. A mistake is not the same thing as the person who did it. When you sever this wrong connection between the deed and the doer, mistakes no longer crumple your self-worth. After you have recognized your mistake, you can do your best to fix it. The less you waste your time and energy on guilt, the more efficient you are in solving the real problem.

If up to this point receiving criticism has caused you a huge drama in one way or another, it is certainly very difficult for you to believe that it could be something this simple. The stronger you are used to thinking that mistakes determine your self-worth, the harder it is for you to adopt this truth. Still, move gradually and with confidence towards this third, more tranquil way. Your quality of life will improve from that move considerably. In *4.10 Properly criticized* we go through this with even more detail.

It is, of course, possible that you are afraid of criticism for the fact that you feel you need other people's approval in order to be happy. Then you dedicate all your energy to pleasing others and you never get to be your authentic self. In addition to wasting life in a "wrong skin," people don't necessarily warm to your pleasing because they think that the most interesting people are people who have found their own authenticity.

Already reading the preceding paragraphs with *insight* will grow your self-worth with huge leaps. Your self-worth will grow further when you learn more about distorted thought patterns, silent assumptions, straightening these distortions, maturation into an authentic adult, and character strengths and virtues of positive people as you read this book further.

You may have already consciously or unconsciously tried to improve your self-worth with a wrong method. Next we have to go through that method and then send it to a hazardous waste disposal facility. The name of this method is improving one's self-worth by belittling others.

Imagine that the height of your self-worth is "three feet." Then imagine next that you have a really good friend and you think that your friend's self-worth is "ten feet high" because he is a really qualified, talented, smart, successful, good-looking, cheerful, and a popular person. A primitive way to strive for equal heights is to attempt to pull your friend from "ten feet" height down to your "three feet" height. In order to do that, you think or even say out loud these kinds of things "But I am still better than he is in mathematics." You waste your energy trying to rake up your otherwise splendid friend's *inadequacies* so that you yourself can feel more worthy. This kind of route is a dangerous route of envy. Sooner or later your friend at least senses that you are pulling him down and you end up without his excellent company. Therefore, notice how you try to lift up your self-worth. The right way is that you yourself rise naturally to that "ten feet" height by loving yourself and by not being boastful, and you don't pull others down to "three feet."

Besides low self-worth, the origin of envy consists of a silent assumption that we live in a very finite world. The universe, however, expands every moment, and water corresponding to a million bathtubs full of water rushes down Niagara Falls every minute. Have you ever wondered why that spewing of water doesn't stop? How on earth has there been enough water corresponding to those one million bathtubs a minute for already about 12,000 years, and the falls don't even show signs of slowing down? If you have never thought about it, it may be that you think from a standpoint of *scarcity*, not *abundance*. Belief in scarcity is emphasized differently in different cultures, and it conditions us to feel that if someone has something then we are automatically left out and without it. Thus, for instance, in Finland, people made magic in the old days at Midsummer in which they seized growth vigor from their neighbor's fields to their own fields by collecting dew. The thought model behind this was that there is only a certain quota of growth vigor, and one must capture his own share even if it meant hurting someone else in the process. It never occurred to those magic makers that there is sufficient growth vigor to be passed on to everyone. It takes an even higher maturity level to think that everyone benefits when everyone is successful. It takes yet even higher maturity level to think that it is for my benefit if my neighbor is successful, even though I myself am not successful right at this moment.

Scarcity with certain things is surely true. For instance, fossil fuels are finite, but that is only a good thing because it is totally senseless to use them when the Sun is shining more energy in one hour on our planet than the whole humanity uses in a year. It would be possible for mankind to solve energy management and other problems that truly limit humanity's success. Hence a silent assumption of scarcity is first and foremost and only in our minds.

Scarcity and abundance share a similar pair of standpoints as fear and trust. People are often motivated with fear, when instead people should be motivated with trust.

If we go back to those "ten feet," what is it like to be up there? Up on that height, the following saying is in force "When you are big, you dare to be small." From "ten feet high," it is already easy to praise and encourage others, rejoice the success of others, admit to one's own mistakes and, if need be, ask for help with an open mind. From that height, one also dares to show one's feelings.

Your self-worth improves when you truly internalize the concept that we all are, from the very beginning, at least at "ten feet high." Ten feet is a constant from the beginning of life until its end. If one thinks himself of being only at "three feet high," one is wrong. That "ten feet high" neither can be worn away shorter, nor can one climb any higher. Even receiving the Nobel Prize won't add the height even for a hundredth of an inch. No matter how you choose to live your life, you always have the same "ten feet" height of self-worth.

A prerequisite for high self-worth is that one loves oneself. When one loves oneself, one also takes a good care of oneself. The thought of loving and caring for oneself may cause confusion in some readers because we have always been warned of self-love. A dictionary gives such synonyms for self-love as egotism, self-importance, self-conceit, and self-glory. For this reason, some people seem to have a misconception that loving oneself is conceited, puffed-up, arrogant, and sick. The fact is, however, that it represents health to treat oneself lovingly without a wrong kind of humility or superiority, fully aware of both one's strengths and weaknesses. Even if all the other people around you place most peculiar conditions in order to love you, you don't set a single condition. You get to love yourself unconditionally, exactly as you are at this very moment.

Loving yourself *is* the master key that opens the door for a healthy self-worth and to maturation into an authentic adulthood and into an authentic self. From this day forward, start your days by saying to yourself that you love yourself. Say it and mean it. If in the beginning you don't believe it, in time you will. Don't give up. Say only shortly that you love you and don't make any additions like "because I'm such a good and compassionate human being." All these extras make your love immediately conditional, but your love towards yourself is completely unconditional. This is under a five second investment that gives an incredible yield.

There is yet a very practical and easy-to-grasp definition for self-worth: *low* self-worth is born when you bully yourself with unreasonable, untrue, and negative thoughts; *fairly high* self-worth sees daylight when you already fight back against these distorted thought patterns; and *high* self-worth is a state at which you have already forced your distortions into a fall. These distortions of thoughts and silent assumptions are dealt with in the next chapters of this book. First you will learn to recognize them and a little later you will learn effective skills for straightening them.

What does even that previous very practical and easy-to-grasp definition of self-worth reveal to you? It, too, tells of love towards oneself. A human heart opens up more and more to love as one's capacity for empathy develops. Thus next we must learn about empathy.

1.3 Empathy

Empathy is an ability to step into someone else's boots and observe the events from the boot-owner's standpoint. It is not necessary to sentimentalize as long as one sees things from the other person's standpoint and understands how that other person feels. This is called *cognitive empathy*. *Affective empathy* includes also an ability to feel as the other person feels. In this case, the person capable of affective empathy has feelings that correspond to the feelings of the person who is the subject of empathy. Those who have *sympathy* feel only their own feelings that prevent sensitivity to the other person's real situation, even though the people who sympathize may be very sorry, worried, and sad on behalf of the other person. Gentle and understanding concern of another person is, in turn, called *support*. Empathy is not sympathy or support. Empathy means that one forgets himself for a moment, and is fictitiously but as truthfully as possible, someone else or even an animal.

In the light of this knowledge, that emotional cousin whom everyone describes as being empathetic may perhaps rather be sympathetic — or perhaps he is both empathetic and sympathetic. This same wonderful cousin is also always ready to support others in the face of adversity. Then on the other hand a slightly standoffish mechanic was clearly empathetic when he showed up with his tools at his neighbor's house to fix his neighbor's car. When he arrived he said: "I figured the breakdown of your car was the last straw for you, since you haven't had it easy lately." The neighbor exclaimed: "That is exactly what I was thinking! I already thought that I'll crawl under the covers and never come out again." Therefore, it is not a question of sentimentalizing, it is not a question of helping either even though this mechanic ended up helping his neighbor, it's a question of stepping into someone else's boots, so that the boots' owner can exclaim: "That is exactly what I was thinking!"

Obtaining a capacity to empathize is not easy. It takes work. In other words, one needs to practice it. An excellent way to improve one's empathic capacity is by imagining and role-playing. Those are methods and methods are not otherwise discussed until in Chapter Four of this book, but imagining and role-playing for improving one's empathic capacity are dealt with here and now. Why? Because improving mankind's capacity to empathize is one of the main objectives of this book. Growth in mankind's empathic capacity is important, if not the most important factor for the survival of this planet and humanity.

Empathy doesn't mean that you have to agree with the person whose standpoint you are using in observing the situation. You only need to see why this other person thinks, says, decides, and acts as he thinks, says, decides, and acts. Therefore, the requirement for empathy is by no means impossible.

You may think that this kind of slipping into someone else's boots doesn't have an effect on anything. In reality empathy is very important for the individuals themselves and for the whole society. When it comes to an individual, empathy is an ingredient of life, which is absolutely essential, if one wishes to mature into an authentic adult. Empathy is important for society because prevailing practices would be much better, fairer, and healthier if all of us improved this noble capacity. How do you think *a lack of empathy* is reflected in your life and in society right now?

You may do role-playing with your friends, but just as well you may have imaginary conversations in your mind in which you place yourself in the situation of your counterparty. If, for instance, you think that your parents should be in a constant preparedness for

providing extra childcare for your children, then have a conversation in your mind in which you play the role of your parents. As you are standing in your parents' boots, start the conversation with, for instance, this kind of line: "You know we love our grandkids. They truly are the saving grace in our lives, and we are happy to take care of them. At the same time, we have dreamt that we could at least sometimes stay at the summer cottage without a break for longer periods of time. Now we don't dare to stay there because you keep us in a constant alert. We worked hard for decades and saved for a long time to get that cottage, but now we just visit there hastily. Could you arrange other options for your extra childcare than just the two of us? We are happy to participate every once in a while, but not all the time."

As your empathic capacity grows, you learn to behave respectfully towards others. The more you practice, the better you become.

Empathy is by far the best antidote for hate. It is therefore a worthwhile effort for everyone who gets easily angry to improve his empathic capacity.

Empathy is also an excellent antidote for the sense of entitlement. The sense of entitlement is based on *controlling others* and *taking away from others*. That is when a person fulfills his own desires without the slightest consideration how it affects other people.

If due to your propensity for anger or sense of entitlement it is easy for you to, for instance, snap at a waiter in a restaurant for the smallest of reasons, then with a developing empathic capacity you will start to observe the situation from the waiter's point of view. You may notice that he has way too many tables to take care of and that he is clearly doing his best.

A role change is also applicable in situations in which the other person's actions seem quite deliberately offensive. This may, for instance, happen in difficult marital disputes. To improve the relationship or even salvage it, it is worthwhile taking the partner's viewpoint and think, why does he always say and act as he always says and acts. If the relationship can't be salvaged, then a role change may at the very least alleviate anger and it will be easier to move on.

1.4 Justice

Justice is relative.

If you think that justice is sharply defined, you have a black-and-white notion. In black-and-whiteness, there is an assumption that we all have more or less similar values, silent assumptions, upbringing, basic education, and so forth. This, however, is not true. There can be a number of totally different viewpoints on a same issue.

A small business owner is furious. He says he has to work also nights and weekends in order to maintain the huge body of civil servants by paying unreasonably high taxes. It sometimes feels to the entrepreneur that due to his heavy workload, he will never make it to his retirement age. *Joie de vivre* has been replaced with toiling forcibly. A civil servant defends himself by saying that when he closed his monitoring eye only for a moment, some milk was contaminated with melamine and tens of thousands of people got seriously ill and some even died. The civil servant continues that people are socially so immature, yet inventive, that if they are not constantly monitored, other members of the society are placed at risk. Which one of them is "right?" The answer is that there is no definitive or universal answer to this question. At least there isn't any black-and-white answer, because there is no absolute justness.

The fact that there's no absolute justice is seen, among other things, from how justice is constantly being weighted in people's conversations, social media, newspapers, and at the different levels of the judicial system. Even though there is no absolute justice, rules and laws are still important and beneficial. In some cases, justice is still clearly defined and hence we, for instance, condemn murder. In some cases, justice has sheer boundaries or a different viewpoint topples the issue totally upside down.

Because justice is relative, then in some cases it would be a sign of wisdom if that same relativity was implemented also for the resolutions and judgments. When a judge asserts strictly to only sections of the law when he weighs up a relative event, then justice is not necessarily realized and certainly not wisdom.

If you think you know what is right and what is wrong, it is possible that you become easily infuriated. You inflame yourself to rage thinking in your mind: "Surely everybody knows what kind of behavior is appropriate in this situation." Most likely the people you are judging act totally "justifiably" from their own point of views.

There is one concession from this relative justice: some people are malicious and without conscience, and their attacks can't be defended by any differences in a viewpoint. That kind of action is unjust as it is.

1.5 Abandonment

Even though you have already adopted the fact of your unchangeable self-worth, your faith will be tested in the moments of abandonment. When someone leaves you, it is easy for you to think once again that you are a failure and a repulsive outcast. Being abandoned is a genuinely painful life experience.

Abandonment may happen throughout the course of one's life. Parents may abandon their children, lovers each other, some friends fall by the wayside, and some beloved ones die.

It is possible for a person to be abandoned even if the abandoner doesn't abandon concretely. This kind of abandonment happens inside the four walls of a home. For instance, a parent may have unreasonable expectations for a child and when those expectations are not met, the parent abandons the child. This doesn't go unnoticed by the child, even if she can't necessarily call it as abandonment. Perhaps even the parent couldn't name it as abandonment. The parent just simply doesn't ever again warm up to his child. The child is left with options to plead constantly for approval through accomplishments, lead an intentionally destructive life after being declared good-for-nothing, or make it through with the support of other loving adults. There may be a lot of grandparents, siblings, aunts, uncles, cousins, teachers, coaches, friends, and neighbors in this world who don't even fathom how they prevented the child from making bad choices due to their support. A gate to a route of destruction was raised through their love and care.

It would require insurmountable maturity on the child's part to see the abandonment as *the parent's own problem*. It would require even more insurmountable maturity of the child to see himself as worthy after such a shocking life experience. These are the points in life when major damages are done. It is never too late, however, to deal with an abandonment that occurred in the childhood (it is never too late to deal with an abandonment that occurred in the adulthood, either). If this happened to you, it is possible for you to cast a new foundation and continue construction again. If you want a steady foundation without wrong types of tilts, you have to adopt the fact that you are always at your full worth. Your worth is *constant* from start to finish.

It definitely helps you in your new construction work to examine the abandonment from the standpoint of the abandoning parent. That is to use empathy. You may do this even though you don't approve the deed. When you stand in the boots of your parent and you have already read this book, you may notice that your parent had a great number of distorted thought patterns and silent assumptions. You may also notice that your parent may not have been socially mature. These observations bring you understanding and at best forgiveness.

Empathy and teachings of distortions, basic human desires and social maturity in the following chapters form a strong cocktail together, and you may use it also when you assess the other parent, who *didn't* abandon. She may have had her own share in the abandonment. Did the parent who stayed have, for instance, a silent assumption that in order to get love, one has to be subservient and with this dependency she tired that other parent who left? What if the abandoning parent never actually abandoned but was merely misjudged in the judicial system? An analytical, rational, unbiased, and a dispassionate mind is ready to consider different options how it all happened as it did. Further understanding helps you move forward.

If you have been abandoned through physical separation, death, or emotional abandonment, it is understandable that it has caused you a lot of pain and sadness. Remember that *no* abandoner is able to take your self-worth with him. You still have it. You only need to take it back into use.

Abandonments happen also in romantic relationships. It is when a girl- or boyfriend or a spouse leaves you. If it happens that your beloved leaves you, the reason is that you weren't in line with his or her personal preferences. It is one hundred percent certain that every single one of us is *wrong* for someone. If your beloved ends up leaving you, it doesn't mean that you are somehow a "bad" person. Neither does it mean that everybody will treat you the same way in the future. By no means should you think that you don't ever want to date again because you will always be abandoned. If you think so, it is called *overgeneralization*, and overgeneralization is one of the distorted thought patterns.

Manipulation can have its own role in abandonments. That is when another person threatens you with abandonment in order to make you behave in a way he or she wants you to behave. Manipulative abandonment may, for instance, sound like this: "Either you do this and this or otherwise I will leave you!" It is equally manipulative to say: "If you don't feel like doing it, then there's a door." If you are made to listen to something along those lines, then the manipulator is trying to control your behavior and compel you under his or her will. That is irrational and destructive. No one has the right to control other people. Because the manipulator himself believes that he has such a right, he is suffering from a fallacy of control, which will be discussed later. The deeper a person is in this fallacy, the more socially immature he is. Social immaturity means being parked at the beginning of the maturation segment. At the same time, that segment is the mental health's segment. There is a way out from that parking spot, and it is offered in this book.

You did your best, but yet your relationship ended. Understandably you go off the rails and wonder how you can ever pull through. First of all, remember that your own thoughts may do the biggest damage. The shock will pass if you persistently refuse to slander yourself. Choose, for instance, a word or a sentence that you will say to yourself every time when you notice you are degrading yourself. Let's assume it is a "cherry blossom." Every time you say cherry blossom to yourself, you stop belittling and blaming yourself on the spot.

After recovering from the initial shock, you hopefully also recognize the possibilities which that abandonment offers to your own maturation. Perhaps it would be worthwhile for you to change some of your thought patterns and habits if they repeatedly play a role in failing your relationships. Maybe it is possible for you to improve your social skills. For instance, don't belittle yourself. Remember also to give sincere compliments to other people and show interest in them. At the same time as you learn from them, they learn from you.

1.6 Guilt

The problem in feelings of guilt is that they are based on distortions. There is always a thought associated with guilt that a person sees himself as bad, evil, vicious, or immoral because he did something he shouldn't have done or he didn't do something he should have done. In truth, the mistake done or the work left undone are only deeds, so it is erroneous to muddle up a deed and a doer to one another. A breadcrumb is not even close to the same thing as a bakery full of loaves, pastries, and cakes. That comparison describes the difference in dimensions between a deed and a doer.

One of the most typical distortion leading to guilt is *personalization*. In other words, you believe incorrectly that you are responsible for other people's feelings, actions, and possibly for the forces of nature. Even a rain shower can cause guilt in some people if it is hits on an important celebratory day. This kind of thinking is associated with a fallacy of control: you are neither supposed to control other people nor forces of nature. When you draw your boundaries of control to be skin-fitting to yourself, as they should be, you relax considerably. At this point, you may defend yourself by saying that, on the contrary, you are selfless, compassionate, and you care about other people. Hopefully you will see a fallacy of control in such thoughts as you keep reading further.

As you remember, a person with low self-worth has magnifying glasses as his eyeglasses. A tendency to magnify is also associated with guilt, because disproportionate intensity, an excessively long duration, and unreasonable consequences are typical for feelings of guilt. An example of unreasonable consequences is punishing oneself for several decades for a fairly insignificant mistake done in the youth.

Because slandering oneself is associated with feelings of guilt, those feelings make a slippery slope down to low-spiritedness or even further down to true depression. A person feeling guilt may also feel ashamed if he wonders what other people think of him. A person feeling guilt may also feel anxiety if he is afraid of a punishment or revenge.

There is no person so severely punished, as those who subject themselves to the whip of their own remorse.

- Lucius Annaeus Seneca

Guilt is also caused by distorted expectations. For instance, a perfectionist may have this fairly typical and unreasonable expectation: "I have to be happy all the time." When a perfectionist has even the slightest case of blues, he thinks he is a failure. This kind of expectation of perfection is doomed to fail in this imperfect world.

Particularly family members and friends of a person who has committed a suicide suffer from guilt. Because feelings of guilt are often very intense in these cases, this is worthwhile being examined more closely.

Those who were close to a person who committed a suicide torture themselves with questions like these: "'Why didn't I prevent it?' 'Why was I so stupid?' 'Why was I so senseless?'" The guilt of the family members and friends may be strengthened by feelings that life delivered themselves better cards from the get-go than to the one who chose the suicide. Quite often the family members and friends have tried to compensate this disadvantage with different kinds of support, sometimes also with financial support.

It may also be excruciating for the family members and friends to know whether they unknowingly contributed somehow to the suicide. That unintentional participation may involve anything from information to material items. For instance, a pharmacist friend may afterwards realize that it was him who gave that relevant piece of information about medication that contributed to carrying out the suicide. That is when the family members and friends may feel as if they themselves were murderers.

Family members and friends describe the situation often like this: "If only I had asked him about his state of mind when he called me. Perhaps I could have rescued him. I was angry with him several times during the last year prior to his death. One time, when I was really irritated, I remember thinking that maybe we should let him die because he constantly went on how he'd be better off dead. Now I feel horribly guilty for those thoughts. Maybe I wanted him to die. I let him down so I deserve to die."

The origin for the feelings of guilt caused by a suicide is nonetheless the above-mentioned distortion, which is called personalization. Family members and friends can, at their best, influence the person brooding over a suicide — and that is what they usually do — but no one can penetrate the other person's mind and shift their negative thoughts into positive. That is a change only a person himself can make.

Furthermore, family members and friends can't know in advance when their loved one ends up committing a suicide. If they knew, they would do their utmost to prevent it. It is unreasonable to presume that anyone is capable of predicting the future.

Even though family members and friends are not responsible for their loved one who ended up choosing a suicide, they are responsible for themselves and their own well-being. If they want to act responsibly, they have to refuse to feel guilt, recover from depression, and strive for reinstating their life satisfaction. That is a responsible action.

Since guilt is distorted, how then to replace it when you have behaved inappropriately, harmfully, or hurtfully? Then it is worthwhile using empathy. When you take the other person's standpoint, you see how your behavior affected him and yourself. The understanding provided by empathy creates appropriate feelings of regret without a need for you to label yourself as a "bad" person. Healthy regret differs from guilt also for the fact that it is reasonable for its intensity, duration, and consequences. When you don't carry unnecessary guilt, you are more relaxed, and it is easier for you to develop a plan by which you may repair the consequences of your objectionable deed, if it is at all possible to repair them. Very often you can at least apologize. That would be fine and respectable behavior.

1.7 Anger

You already read from the previous sections that if you have a rigid view of justice, you most probably get easily infuriated. You may have thought so far that, for instance, difficult, incompetent, and indifferent people, unpleasant world events, politics, and bureaucracy make you angry. In reality, you yourself make you angry. How so? Because the situation always demands your interpretation first, that is to say your thoughts, before you feel any degree of anger. Even when something genuinely dreadful happens, there is first a phase when you determine a value of enragement for that situation. It works greatly for your benefit to understand and accept that you are responsible for setting a degree for your anger. It then means that you have an opportunity to manage it.

When Ryan is late for train, he explodes. When Evan is late for train, he is really annoyed, but he doesn't explode. The difference is that Ryan's value for being late is "ten" and Evan's "six" on the same scale of getting enraged. They themselves set the values for the external event that was exactly the same for both of them.

More often than not your anger doesn't help you. You merely trample on the same spot or at worst you destroy. It would be wiser if you invested your precious resources in finding creative solutions: what can you do to remedy the situation or could you do something, so that you won't run into a similar situation ever again?

If I know Ryan and Evan at all, I presume that Ryan only thinks negative consequences and is peevish until the departure of the next train or even until next week. He uses his energy also in finding and naming the guilty party, and he is able to talk about them with contempt even next Christmas. Evan, instead, starts to see very soon the virtues of his mishap. Perhaps both Ryan and Evan have to first make some calls to explain the situation to their employers or family members who are affected by this delay. After that Evan decides to make a good use of the time he has before the departure of the next train. For once he has the time, for instance, to go to that specialty store he has dreamt of visiting for quite some time. Alternatively, in high spirits and in peace, he decides to enjoy a cup of coffee and read the daily newspaper.

Typically, it is very difficult for the people who become easily angry to accept that their own thinking is distorted because they have nearly an irresistible desire to always blame others and retaliate. How does this apply to you? Do you defuse your anger into revenge? Your revenge doesn't help you to get to a meaningful resolution, but exactly the opposite. Even if you temporarily get your way, your instant win will later cost you dearly in one way or another. Sub-chapter *4.10 Properly criticized* may prove to be golden for you.

Once again empathy is of great help. Empathy rounds off the sharpest edges of anger. You understand better the different kinds of situations and you see your own share in them. You dare to carry responsibility because admitting to your own share no longer means that you are a failure as a human being. You are not a failure because you already know that you are valuable and you can keep the deed apart from the doer. With empathy you may come down in your anger from "ten" to, for instance, "seven." That would already be reasonable.

1.8 Grief

Grief is a normal emotional state due to loss, disappointment, or other misfortune. There are no distorted thought patterns in grief. Grief doesn't include lowering of one's self-worth. Grief also has a reasonable duration.

When, for instance, someone close to you dies, you rightfully think: "I have lost him. I tremendously miss his company." Feelings that are born from such undistorted thinking are affectionate, reality-based, and desirable.

This book handles grief very little because grief is a normal, pure, and undistorted emotion, and the interest in this book is rather in distortions of thoughts and silent assumptions and how to get rid of them. People who struggle with prolonged grief are, however, offered the following scheduling method.

> Schedule one or more moments in your day — five to ten minutes at a time is probably sufficient — when you think of sad, angry, and desperate thoughts that are connected to your loss, disappointment, adversity, or separation. Cry, bewail, bemoan, and pound a pillow if need be. When the time ends, stop, and continue with your normal life until the next scheduled moment. This kind of scheduling can speed the grieving process and bring it to a completion.

Other person's sympathy, that is to say, his attempt to feel sorrow by your side, doesn't always help. In some research, it was shown that sympathy may even extend the grieving period.

1.9 Depression

When depression is compared to grief, depression is always connected with distorted thought patterns. When someone dear and close dies, a depressed person may think along these lines: "This is unfair. I can never be happy again. I can't stand this." These kinds of thoughts are based on distortions and generate self-pity and hopelessness. Depression has also a tendency to recur for an indefinite period of time. Furthermore, there is always a lowering of self-worth in depression.

When the underlying cause for depression is an apparent stress as, for instance, illness, death of someone close, or a financial setback, it is sometimes referred to as *reactive depression*. Depression, which, in turn, seems to come into existence from nowhere, is called *endogenous depression*. In both cases the cause however is the same: distorted, negative thought patterns, and silent assumptions. When distortions have been straightened, getting over "the real problem" is easier.

When a person is stricken with a serious physical illness, he doesn't necessarily sink into depression, although it is often assumed so. If a person with a serious physical illness does, however, get depressed, and he is asked to describe what inflames his emotions most, his answers are often along these lines: "I will never reach my goals. I can't and I am too tired to participate in all the fun activities. I am a burden to my family." Those answers reveal a silent assumption that a person's worth is measured based on his accomplishments. When a serious illness takes an ability to accomplish, a person feels he is ballast. You already read from *1.2 Self-worth and self-esteem* that a person's worth is constant throughout the course of his life, and it has nothing to do with accomplishments. Thus an ill person doesn't need to earn his worth. When an ill person truly realizes and accepts this truth, he often recovers very quickly from his depression.

A person who loses a limb or a sense may assume that the limitations set by his physical injury mean unavoidably lowered ability for him to be happy. More often than not the depression is generated from distorted thoughts rather than the injury itself. A person who has lost a limb or a sense and who is also depressed may focus all his thinking on things he no longer can do and enjoy. You will learn from the next chapter that the name for this kind of distorted thinking is *mental filter*. A person picks only a negative detail from an experience or a situation and seizes solely upon that, whereupon he thinks that the whole experience or situation is unpleasant. The best treatment for this kind of a depressed person may be that he has to list all the possible activities he *can* still participate in and enjoy.

A great number of people feel that when one is unemployed it corresponds to being declared good-for-nothing. There is a Western view behind this that a person's worth and ability to be happy is linked directly with professional success. Then it seems obvious and rational that a foundered career and financial loss lead inevitably to depression. The truth is here too, however, that there is no equal sign between financial worth and human worth. Being unemployed and the consequent impoverishment don't reduce slightest the worth of a human being. The worth of a human being is always constant, no matter the circumstances.

It is also worthwhile for a depressed person to keep in mind that the slowness and procrastination he is experiencing are symptoms of depression, not manifestations of a true self. Depression is a temporary disorder, and it is only after recovery that a person's true self is able to come out.

Depression is still further discussed in the following chapters of this book.

1.10 Relinquishment

In order for a person to grow and mature, he needs to give up something once in a while. This kind of relinquishment can be, say, giving up a difficult trait. If, for instance, a person notices that his desire to be always the best expels other people, he may decide to give up his compulsion to win. Quite often depression is involved in these moments of relinquishment. Thus periods of depression of some degree are completely natural and healthy to a maturing human being. Depression is unhealthy when something disrupts this process of relinquishment. It may, for instance, be disrupted by the fact that, as a child, one was forced to give up something or lost something before he was ready for it, and this has caused an oversensitivity to relinquishment and loss. However, a person can little by little sensitize himself again to the noble capacity of relinquishing.

A large proportion of people have a silent assumption that everything was much better before. Even from their depression they would want to return to a situation that preceded their disorder. It is a law of nature, however, that life is constantly changing, and there is no return to the same old same old. In other words, one also has to give up situations and circumstances that existed in the past. Once a person accepts nature's law of constant change, life becomes significantly easier.

In everyone's growth and maturation, there are moments of collective relinquishment and relinquishment that pertains to one's personal life. For instance, at some point all of us have to give up our beliefs that concern our parents. When one accepts the limitations of one's parents, it brings understanding and forgiveness. Becoming adult means also giving up the care included in the childhood because adulthood pertains taking responsibility. A parent, in turn, has to give up his position of authority towards his adult child. Ageing brings along all kinds of relinquishment. If the attitude towards relinquishing is accepting and understanding, life becomes easier.

Sometimes it is worthwhile to consciously discard some of the accumulated material things. Giving up excessive and needless material things can be thought of as a refreshing and purifying way to shed one's skin. Hence the abandonment of matter does not automatically represent loss and failure.

It, too, is relinquishment that when a person is learning and experiencing something new, he gives up his old limiting thoughts and opens up. Way too many people don't implement even this momentary relinquishment, but instead they examine new information with relentless skepticism. This kind of person thinks of himself as being selective and sensible, but in reality he is often a person who doesn't want to evolve. This kind of strong resistance may bring a greater limitation to learning than the limitations brought by intelligence. Friction is so great that it would require unreasonable force to progress very far.

A brave and evolving human being also dares to give up momentarily his sense of well-being in order to move onto the next step in his recovery and maturation, as recognizing one's shortcomings, outdated silent assumptions, and distorted thought patterns may cause pain. This kind of mental pain is healthy maturation pain no one should fear. However, there are plenty of those who do. When the avoidance of pain is added to the unwillingness to work for one's maturation, we get those who externalize their own maturation. Examples of such are parents who want their children to fulfill their own dreams. These parents want to live vicariously through their children, and they deceive themselves by thinking that they act "in the child's best interest."

Life can be seen as a staircase of relinquishment or a hurdle track of relinquishment. Those who think life is a staircase of relinquishment get an opportunity to admire the landscape from higher positions as they dare to climb still only higher. Those who think life is a hurdle track of relinquishment, resist every hurdle and try to forcefully remain firmly in a place — "I wish everything was as it used be."

This section about relinquishment was deliberately positioned already in the beginning part of this book so that your mind is open for the next chapters.

1.11 Surprising brains

Next there is a reason to dispel some deep-rooted ideas about a brain.

Especially people of older generations have learned that nerve cells don't regenerate, and that a brain is a very stable, unchanging organ. Another deep-rooted idea is that intelligence doesn't improve after youth. In other words, the level we are labeled with at school is true and determines the rest of our lives. This is *not* true.

If we strongly believe in our silent assumptions, then they become true. If one believes that an adult brain remains unchanged, that is how it remains, for example, for a cerebral infarction patient, who due to this silent assumption doesn't train during convalescence. He thinks that the repeatable, simple tasks are completely pointless, and therefore he does them only haphazardly. Another cerebral infarction patient, who has had an exactly identical injury, believes that the brain is flexible and new parts of it will take over the functions of the damaged area as long as his brain receives persistent training. This second patient is ultimately much more capable of functioning than the first patient who had that different kind of silent assumption.

A brain is in many respects malleable even in an adult, and the changes are reliably measurable. Research shows that, amongst other things, empathy changes the structure of a brain. It has been demonstrated that people who are capable of empathy have cerebral gray matter that is denser in some parts of the brain than people who are incapable of empathy. You have already learned that empathy is a skill that can be learned. With practice, a brain literally configures itself to a new form.

Brain research has also demonstrated that people who meditate have more gray brain cells and better neural connections between different parts of a brain than people who do not meditate. Veteran meditators have also a cerebral cortex that has more folds than that of non-meditators. This kind of strong folding is associated with better data processing. In addition, in the brains of those who meditate regularly, aging-induced atrophy is slower. As well as

a capacity for empathy, also meditation is a skill that can be fully learned. In Chapter Four of this book, there is a short introduction to meditation, which opens gateways for brain modification.

You read from above that bibliotherapy can heal one from negativity and depression. What then happens in a brain? The read and adopted text and therapy changes brain chemistry and even the brain's neural connections. Maybe you didn't previously believe — or perhaps you have never even thought about it — that a brain is malleable to such a large extent by our own thoughts and by the thought breaks generated during meditation. This is really encouraging news for you.

Many consider a depressive disorder as a chemical imbalance in the brain and then medication has been seen as a solution. As you read from above, *thoughts* alter brain chemistry. Thoughts indeed generate chemistry! If you keep thinking the same thoughts that generated that chemical imbalance, you keep generating that same old chemical imbalance. Then medication doesn't, properly speaking, cure, but it only fights to keep the chemistry at least in some kind of equilibrium. If you truly want to cure the disorder and not simply cover the symptoms, you need to work on your thoughts so that they generate healthy chemistry.

When you build new chemistry and new neural connections with the help of your new thoughts and new thought breaks, keep in mind that the raw materials for these new molecules continue coming from outside of you, that is from the food you eat. You have to feed your chemical manufacturing plant with genuine and real food. With proper nutrition, the right kinds of thoughts, and appropriate thought breaks, it is possible for you to become your own best pharmacy.

2 Distorted thought patterns

When a person thinks negative thoughts, there are distortions of thinking in the background. If you think negatively, you may present objection that there is no defect in your thinking. You say that you have real life problems and the negative thoughts come along forcibly with those. Perhaps you are unemployed, bankrupt, divorced, lonesome, or you are being treated poorly. You may also think that you are unhappy because you are not "enough of anything," like sufficiently talented, hard-working, or good-looking. You may also think that other people are to blame for your problems or that your negativity stems from having bad genes. Therefore, you may come to a conclusion that there is nothing you can do about your negative thoughts for real.

You are both right and wrong. You are right that grief is always involved in hardships. Grief and depression are, however, different things, as you already read from the previous chapter. There are no distortions in grief. Grief is a pure emotion. If you think that there is nothing you can do about your negative and depressive thoughts, then in that assumption you are, however, wrong.

Reading this book will not remove existing or future setbacks from your life. This book helps you in the way you face these setbacks. Successful change will bring you energy with which you can solve those real life problems. Perhaps your real life problems require a visit at a debt advisor, employer, labor broker, relative, attorney, civil servant, bank manager, realtor, priest, headmaster, physician, therapist, nutritionist, or personal trainer. Perhaps you can find a solution from the internet. Whatever your real life problem is, you can better attend to solutions when distortions are no longer taxing your strength.

If you would like to know the degree of your depression before you get started, you may take a depression test on the internet. These kinds of depression tests are, for example, the Beck Depression Inventory (BDI), the Montgomery-Åsberg Depression Rating Scale (MADRS), the Zung Self-Rating Depression Scale, and the Hamilton Rating Scale for Depression (HRSD or HAM-D). The test result is quite trustworthy because these very same tests are used in professional health care.

One of the goals in this book is to encourage you to be *your own life's researcher*. As part of this goal, you may want to take a depression test and repeat the same test later when you have read this book to the end. You may test yourself also at other stages of your life. The result is always a message of something, and that message should be interpreted and conclusions drawn — like an own life's researcher does.

If you took the depression test and it showed that you are mildly depressed, you have no cause for alarm. It is nonetheless worthwhile to remedy, and you will make significant progress with the help of this book. Very often especially those who are mildly depressed may have suffered for years or even throughout their lifetime. A mild depression which goes on and on is called *dysthymia*. A person with dysthymia is gloomy, negative, and unresponsive for most of the time. Fortunately, the methods presented in this book help also in these mild, chronic depressions.

If according to a test you have a moderate depression and your condition remains substantially the same for more than two weeks, seek to meet a professional in the mental health sector. He has been trained to help exactly you.

If your depression is severe or even very severe, your suffering may already be almost unbearable. This definitely requires seeing a professional in the mental health sector and his suggestions for the treatment program. As a spark of hope, I want to leave you with a result from research-based evidence: sometimes the most severe depressions react fastest to the treatment. As it was stated in the beginning: psychotherapy, drug therapy, and bibliotherapy are not contradictory, but support each other. Bibliotherapy may speed up the healing process significantly. This, too, is an outcome from research.

It is worthwhile to point out that depression may produce physical symptoms, which in turn raise concern for one's state of physical health. Such uncomfortable physical symptoms are, among others, constipation, diarrhea, pain, insomnia, or a need for excessive sleeping, fatigue, dizziness, tremors, and numbness. As a person heals from a depression, these physical symptoms in all likelihood disappear. To be sure an opposite situation is, however, also quite possible because a number of treatable physical illnesses may first show up as depression. Therefore, observe your situation against this information.

2.1 Sixteen distorted thought patterns

Negative thinking patterns are universal, that is to say that people think in a similarly distorted way apparently in all corners of the planet. Pioneers in cognitive psychotherapy developed a collection of distorted thought patterns under the direction of psychiatrist *Aaron Beck*. Larger audiences became familiar with them through the book *Feeling good* by psychiatrist David D. Burns. A great deal of credit goes also to the very first pioneers, Drs. *Abraham Lowe* and *Albert Ellis*.

Originally the collection had ten distorted thought patterns, but it has grown since then. From published literature and from internet sources, it is possible to find even 50 distorted thought patterns. A collection of sixteen thought patterns ended up in this book, and it will be outlined next.

There is a reference to *narcissism* in the context of some of the distorted thought patterns. At this point, it is worthwhile giving only a very brief description of narcissism: a narcissist has not developed an ability to view things from other people's standpoints, that is, he doesn't feel empathy or he feels it only little. When he uses only his own standpoint, a narcissist thinks of his own interest in a pronounced way, and he usually doesn't hesitate to exploit other people.

It would be beneficial for you to learn the distorted thought patterns on some level because their recognition is "the thing" in cognitive psychotherapy. At this moment the best act of love towards yourself is to read carefully through the descriptions for these thought distortions and reflect upon how they affect you and those close to you. The next act of love towards yourself is to learn how to straighten them from your thinking. I have unwavering confidence that you can do it.

The sixteen distorted thought patterns have the following names:
1. **all-or-nothing thinking**
2. **overgeneralization**
3. **mental filter**
4. **disqualifying the positive**
5. **jumping to conclusions**
6. **magnification or minimization**
7. **emotional reasoning**
8. **should statements**
9. **labeling**
10. **personalization**
11. **blaming**
12. **always being right**
13. **fallacy of change**
14. **fallacy of control**
15. **fallacy of fairness**
16. **fallacy of heaven's reward**

1. All-or-nothing thinking

If you are an all-or-nothing thinker, your world is black-and-white. A technical term for this kind of error of observation is *dichotomous thinking*.

Favorite words for an all-or-nothing thinker are *always, every, never ever,* and *never.* "I always make wrong choices!" "Every time I try something, things go wrong." "I never ever succeed in anything." "I get never picked to a team."

When, for instance, you prepare a three-course dinner, but the dessert turns out to be slightly runnier than was intended, you think the whole dinner is ruined. Because you yourself are the cook, you may also berate yourself: "I am a completely failed human being!" Consequently, everything is black in color, and that black spreads from the courses to the cook as well. In reality you prepared two courses that were greatly successful and one that was slightly unsuccessful. If this was described in colors, you made two white courses and one that was pale grey.

A person seeking perfection, that is, *a perfectionist* may especially fall into black-and-white thinking. A person seeking perfection is often an "A" student to whom a B+ in a test feels like a shame. A perfect "A" represents white, everything below that is directly black.

You read from above that all-or-nothing thinking affects also one's idea of justice. One thinks that matters are either clearly right or clearly wrong, even though in real life justice is relative. You also read from above that an all-or-nothing thinker gets easily angry due to this angular notion of justice. Justice is imperfect. The same applies to real life. It, too, is imperfect. One can find imperfection in everything if one chooses to embark on the road of finding imperfections.

If you are inflexible and demand always perfection, then you are constantly depressed because your severity towards yourself and others does not adapt to this imperfect real life. Your belief in yourself is constantly wavering, because whatever you do, it never reaches to the level of your oversized expectations.

2. Overgeneralization

Overgeneralization means that if something happened to you once in a certain way, you assume that in the future it always happens that same way.

"I didn't pass the driving test, so I will never pass the driving test." "I didn't have any friends in the previous place, so I won't have any friends in the future, no matter where we'll move."

Overgeneralization occurs for instance in moments of abandonment. You conclude that since you were abandoned by your first boy- or girlfriend, you will never want to date again because you will always be abandoned. As you can see, overgeneralization is a distorted thought pattern, which, at its worst, can have a huge impact on the rest of your life. It would be sad if great decisions in your life were based on distortions.

What makes a person overgeneralize? It is fear. In addition to the fear of abandonment, another source for fear is failing. "If I fail in this, it means that I will fail in everything."

Proverbs urge to caution after an unsuccessful experience, but even they don't suggest an extreme attitude in which one unsuccessful experience would better suffice for the rest of one's life time. Thus, for example, and English proverb states: "Once bitten, twice shy." An overgeneralizer's proverb would sound like this: "Once bitten gets always bitten."

3. Mental filter

You pick one unpleasant detail from a situation or experience and cling exclusively to it, in which case you view the whole situation or experience as unpleasant.

Let's assume that you have been invited to a local library to give a presentation about your unusual hobby. Delighted you oblige. In the middle of your presentation, you notice that one member of the audience gets up and leaves. After your presentation, however, several members from the audience commend you profusely for being so inspirational. You don't enjoy the praise because you feel sad for that one audience member leaving in the middle of everything. Even on the next day, you ponder why that one person left. Was the introduction too long after all?

Your mental filter is also on when you interpret everything another person says or does on the basis of a preconception. Then your mental filter is that preconception. Everything has to run through that filter, which gives its own coloring on everything. Let's assume that in the beginning of a relationship you constantly fear that your girlfriend (or boyfriend) will leave you. When she says that she will spend the coming weekend with her parents at their summer cottage, you think that she does so, because she is preparing to leave you. Besides being a mental filter, this case could have also been placed under *jumping to conclusions*.

When exchange students leave abroad, they are asked to take off their colored eyeglasses. Even this represents a mental filter and the request is to leave that filter behind. What is meant is that exchange students should not constantly compare conditions in their destination country to the conditions in their home country, but instead stay open to new experiences. Continuous comparison takes an enormous amount of energy and poisons the experience. With the colored eyeglasses on, one would have to constantly wonder: "Help, do those people wear shoes even inside? In *my* country no one wears shoes inside their homes, that's for sure." "Oops, the washing cycle is less than half an hour! There's no way you can get clean clothes like that. *Our* washing machines wash for a much longer time."

4. Disqualifying the positive

If in the previous mental filter section all positives went unnoticed, even that is not enough in this case, because a depressed person changes also positive into negative and unpleasant. This is also called "reverse alchemy," where precious gold is turned into cheap and heavy lead.

A person, who disqualifies the positive, is talking when you hear the following kind of sentence: "That was a whim of a chance. That can't be taken into account." By saying something along those lines, the nullifier of the positive is able to maintain his negative view even when it is contradictory with the truth. Everyone has probably experienced such a nullification of positive in either their own way or in someone else's way of receiving compliments. If you disqualify the positive, you may nullify a compliment with a light swipe by saying, for instance, something like this: "Oh no, I was pretty crappy." You may continue the nullifying by thinking: "He said that just to be nice." In other words, first you nullify yourself, then also the one who praises you.

While this distorted thought pattern is very common, it also forms the basis for the most difficult forms of depression to be treated.

5. Jumping to conclusions

Do you jump to negative conclusions that are not supported by facts? This kind of hasty jumping to conclusions exists in two different forms, that is, as "mind reading" and "the fortune teller error."

In *mind reading*, you think that you know what other people are thinking. At worst, the consequence is that you make major life decisions merely on the basis of an illusion. Mind reading is, among others, a classic way to start a family dispute. A quarrel can get its ignition, for instance, because a spouse is tired and silent, but the mind reader assumes that he is angry. Instead of a quarrel (or silent treatment), the right approach would be to check out what it going on. All that could be easily cleared up by asking! Usually the reason for "mind reading" is that a person feels he is worthless, and he assumes that other people, too, think he is worthless.

In *the fortune teller error*, you are a fortune teller who insists that things are not going to work out. You are also totally convinced that your predictions are completely true. A depressed person predicts that he will always stay depressed, so that he has to give up his job or his firm. Unfortunately, a fortune teller adds to his own misery with his predictions. In reality, many depressed people have been faced with a realization after their recovery that they were wrong.

This is perfect spot for a Taoist tale of a farmer:

> In ancient China a poor farmer's mare ran away, which made the farmer's neighbors lament: "Oh, what a tragedy!" The farmer said just calmly: "Who knows." After some time, the mare came back with a wild stallion. Neighbors commented: "You were right. It was a stroke of luck after all!" Again the farmer stated calmly: "Who knows." After a while the farmer's son flew off the back of the wild stallion and broke his leg. Neighbors stated: "You were right. What a tragedy!" The farmer repeated as usual: "Who knows." Very soon after this, all the young men of the village were ordered to go to a war. Men of that village were forced to the forefront and none survived. The only young man spared in the village was the farmer's son, because he had his leg broken at the time of the mobilization. The neighbors stated: "You were right. It was a stroke of luck."

In this tale the conclusions drawn by the neighbors don't even seem very hastily made because they had quite convincing evidence before they labeled the situation either fortunate or unfortunate. If even these neighbors were wrong, how likely is it that your conclusion, which is hastily made and based on illusion, is correct?

The actual teaching of this Taoist tale is not connected to jumping to conclusions or only for the part of the farmer being too wise of a man to draw *any* conclusions. The actual teaching of this tale pertained wisdom, humility, and courage. Wisdom is that we don't know our future, humility is to adapt to the unknown, and courage is to react calmly to whatever life brings us.

6. Magnification or minimization

In this distortion, one exaggerates or reduces things. Depressed people usually exaggerate negative things, such as and in particular, their own mistakes and weaknesses and belittle positive things, especially their own strengths. A narcissist, instead, usually exaggerates his own strengths and depreciates others. By this way a narcissist attempts to control other people and tries to improve his own self-worth with a method we already sent to a hazardous waste disposal facility in subsection *1.2 Self-worth and self-esteem.*

This distortion has a separate subclass called "catastrophizing," which means exaggerating a situation into a catastrophe. "Terrible! I made a staggeringly huge mistake! My reputation is gone!" In this case, the distortion is in expecting the worst possible outcome, even though it is highly unlikely it would ever materialize. The consequence is that the situation is seen as unbearable, when it really is only uncomfortable.

Behind anxiety there is usually exaggeration. Anxiety is one of the most common psychological problems. It is estimated that up to 5% of people under 18 years of age experience anxiety, which is so intense that they would need outside help. Anxiety is a normal feeling that sometimes bothers everyone. Anxiety is, however, abnormal when it visits often, restricts life, and is intense. When anxiety strikes, the other person's well-intentioned comforting often makes the situation only worse because it strengthens the anxious person's notion that the world is, indeed, an evil and dangerous place. If you are anxious, do you recognize exaggeration in your thoughts?

A belittler may easily let it slip from his mouth: "I can't do it." There may be a fear that otherwise he is seen as inefficient. The problem in this defense is that, in the end, the belittler himself believes in this explanation. Even though we are only at the introduction stage of the distorted thought patterns, I already suggest to the belittlers out there: remind yourself of the tasks you did during a day and give praise to yourself for each and every one of them. This helps you to pay attention to things you have done, instead of fretting all the time what you haven't done. This may sound simple, but it works.

7. Emotional reasoning

Emotional reasoning means that you let your feelings decide what you should do. If you feel miserable and anxious, you assume automatically and erroneously that the work or leisure activity you had planned is miserable.

A person, who bases his truth on his feelings, may say: "I'm in such a lousy mood, I feel like doing nothing. It's best that I stay in bed." Postponing work and inefficiency are the most typical consequences of emotional reasoning. The shocking truth, however, is this: first is action and that leads to motivation.

Learn to observe situations where you have erroneously concluded that your feelings stand for the truth. Let's say that you don't want to go to a floorball practice because your miserable mood claims that floorball is a pretty miserable hobby. Your friend, however, manages to tempt you to come along and after the practice you are really pleased that you went because you enjoyed playing very much. Notice situations like this and learn from them. Remind yourself also afterwards: "Even then I assumed beforehand erroneously, but then I went and I had a lot of fun. Maybe the same happens this time as well."

Emotional reasoning has a strong contribution to depression. Hence this distortion is worthwhile focusing on.

8. Should statements

"I should go to the gym." "I shouldn't have eaten that chocolate." When you say such "should" statements, you think you are motivating yourself. In reality you only feel guilty and miserable. Quite often it also happens that the tasks with such a "should" label on them start to feel unappealing. When you postpone doing them, you label yourself lazy and your mood drops even further.

The problem in "should" statements would be small if it was only limited to this drop in one's mood. "Should" statements have, however, a bigger problem. If you keep cultivating them, you reveal at the same time that you think that you should always be perfect, omniscient, and omnipotent. That is a totally impossible expectation in this imperfect world. If you are so hard on yourself, you end up getting constantly disappointed.

You may also target "should" statements on other people. Then you reveal that you feel that you have the right to make things run exactly according to your script. You may, for instance, think that your guests *should* be standing during the beginning toast and speeches in your party, but to your disappointment, some guests are sitting. Internally you are positively fuming that there is this non-compliance with your unspoken rule.

In reality it is not true that you have the right to get what you want and only because you want it. We all are different, and we have different values and habits. Thus it is worthwhile for you to adjust your expectations. It is also worthwhile for you to learn some negotiation skills. It is way easier to change self to fit into this world than to try to change this world to fit oneself.

Different methods for removing "should" statements are presented in Chapter Four. At this point you could already try replacing "should" with expressions like "it would be nice if…" or "I wish I could…" or "I have an opportunity…" These kinds of expressions are more truthful, and they don't generate the same kind of mental turmoil as that prickly "should."

Don't, however, be totally afraid of using "should" in the future, because it also has a positive side. You may say to your friend on the phone: "We really should meet." You probably mean that you would love to meet your friend, and you have truly longed for his good company.

9. Labeling

Labeling means that you also label a doer negatively based on a negative deed. You may give such a label on yourself or someone else. However, you learned already from subchapter *1.2 Self-worth and self-esteem* that a deed and a doer shouldn't be mixed to one another in any circumstances. That kind of thinking is distorted.

Labeling is considered as an extremist form of overgeneralization. In overgeneralization, a negative deed or event means that all the following deeds and evens are also negative. In labeling, one doesn't just hold onto mere deeds and events with their offspring, but also the doer is added into the same soup.

Most likely you engage yourself in labeling if you describe your mistakes with sentences that begin with "I am ..." If, for instance, you get a fine for your parking, you reproach yourself: "How could I be that stupid!" The truth is that you only made a mistake that you can handle by paying the fine.

If you are a labeler, you think that you are a failure when you procrastinate. The more you procrastinate, the bigger "loser" you think you are. This lowers your self-confidence even further. Hence labeling works as a means to mill huge blocks off of one's self-confidence.

If you are a labeler, you naturally label others as well. If your spouse makes a dumb deed, you think your spouse is dumb. In reality, your spouse only did dumbly. When you immediately magnify a deed to include its doer, your hate gauge hits red, and it is a long distance from up there down to composure. This tendency to label is one of the reasons why you overreact in disputes.

Labeling is irrational. When a doer is "one hundred percent" in existence during his life course, one deed represents a "per mil" of the entire life course, if even that. In other words: if a doer is thought to be, say, a twelve-story ocean liner, then one insulting, harmful, or detrimental deed is that ocean liner's lifeboat's seat number 134. If a seagull poops on the seat number 134, no one says that the ocean liner is a pigsty and definitely ruined. Even you wouldn't claim that that ocean liner is ruined, but you insist so in your own case.

10. Personalization

A person who suffers from this distortion feels guilty when someone — usually a family member — doesn't act as expected or doesn't do that well. Guilt makes this distortion sufferer intervene too much with another person's life, though he may defend himself by saying that he is just trying to support and help. Behind this kind of thinking is an incorrect mixing up of *influencing* other people with *controlling* other people. In a role as a parent, spouse, friend, therapist, teacher, judge, priest, physician, nurse, pharmacist, sales professional, civic activist, personal trainer and so on, a person surely influences the people who he is dealing with, but he has no right to control them. What the other person ultimately does is his own responsibility.

You may get a realization that maybe another adult should not be controlled, but surely a child must be controlled. It is only a child after all! In reality no one should be controlled. Not even a child. A child, who is controlled, realizes the life of his controller, not his own. Everyone on this planet has come here to realize their own life. That is the meaning of life. Of course a child's well-being has to be guaranteed, he has to be loved, he has to be accepted as he is, and he has to have an order, boundaries, and guidance in his life. You may have confused setting boundaries to being controlled. They are, however, different things.

Description of personalization has been later extended to cover also that kind of personalization in which one believes that everything other people say has something to do with him. Such a person can be convinced, for instance, that a group of friends or acquaintances is discussing some famous singer's fantastic singing voice only to ridicule, between the lines, his own weak singing voice. In addition, such a personalizer constantly compares himself to others and tries to determine who in the group is the most intelligent, beautiful, successful, wealthy, and so forth. He is very keen on knowing how he rates to other members in a group.

There is also "taking something personally." That is used when for instance an employer is trying to advise and guide an employee, but the employee feels offended. The employee "takes it personally."

What is that then all about? In this case the employee feels that the criticism is directed at him as a person. He feels that the employer sees him as a failure. The problem is the same as in labeling, that is, the employee feels offended because he himself mixed a deed and a doer to one another. When one learns to keep the deed and the doer separate from each other, it brings peace of mind, but it also brings a better ability to learn as this is when one is able to receive guidance with an open mind.

11. Blaming

In this distortion pattern, one blames other people for the discomfort or mischief they experience. Other people may have, indeed, contributed in generating that discomfort or mischief, either intentionally or unintentionally, but the blamer doesn't see at all his own involvement in the issue. This is a narcissistic trait.

The most typical example is when a wife or a husband blames exclusively the spouse and is completely blind to her or his own mistakes. A person who suffers from this blaming distortion doesn't see how he with his own words and acts has also contributed to the fact that the relationship is running aground.

12. Always being right

Some people think they are always right. Then the pursuit for one's own advantage and selfishness prevail over other people's feelings. This, too, is a narcissistic trait.

A person suffering from this distortion gets irritated or goes even berserk if someone dares to challenge him. Because the sufferer of this distortion believes he is always right, he can't give in during disagreements, but instead continues relentlessly with his own argumentation. If the dispute is ended such that the adversaries agree together to disagree, the sufferer of this distortion has to be left with a notion that he was more right. If there is a general understanding that the sufferer of this distortion was wrong, he continues arguing.

Unfortunately, it is difficult for an "always being right" person to change because he doesn't see anything wrong with himself. After all, he is always right.

13. Fallacy of change

Have you been called a "prima donna?" Do you expect that your spouse doesn't attend an event either if you simply don't feel like going? Do you expect that other people arrange their schedules according to yours? Is compromise a foreign word to you? If you answered "yes," you may suffer from this distortion.

A person who suffers from this distortion believes sincerely that another person or other people have to change in order for him to feel happy. Naturally the previous blaming distortion is closely connected to this fallacy of change.

In this distortion pattern, a person is blind to the fact that happiness stems from oneself. A person's unhappy existence is the end result of one's *own thoughts*. Therefore, the object for the change has to be the person himself.

A source of happiness for a narcissist is exclusively in other people. Because narcissists believe that happiness comes from the outside, they exert pressure or flattery or both of them to achieve their goals. Their goals, however, remain always only as a mirage on a desert, unless they open their eyes to the truth.

14. Fallacy of control

In this book controlling refers primarily to treating other people as one's own play-dough. Then a person thinks he has the right to shape others, so they comply with his wishes. Controlling means also interfering in things, which obviously do not belong to oneself. In addition, controlling is behaving in an excessive way when giving guidance and monitoring compliance to rules. A usual provision of guidance, monitoring of compliance, setting boundaries, and so forth, represents, instead, normal management, parenting, or leadership.

A person has the right to control only himself. He is also expected to control himself.

Fallacy of control means that one thinks he can control *more* than is truthful or, alternatively, he can control *less* than is truthful.

Too much control is involved, among others, in personalization, which was already discussed in the set of ten original distorted thought patterns above. Many of those suffering from a personality disorder, for instance, a narcissist, also exert too much control.

Because of a feeling of too little control, a person doesn't believe he can contribute in any way, even though he could and it is even expected of him. Due to too little control, a person may, for instance, blindly rely on his family members, friends or experts, and leave himself completely at their mercy. At this point you may ask yourself: "To whom am I or my case more important, to myself or to other people?"

15. Fallacy of fairness

In this fallacy, a person is often angry because other people don't share his sense of justice. In the original set of ten distorted thought patterns, this thought distortion was already included in all-or-nothing thinking.

16. Fallacy of heaven's reward

According to this thought distortion, good deeds and self-denial lead to a reward. When there is no reward, disappointment and indignation follow.

Doing good deeds is noble. The only problem is the rule connected to it: "When I do good deeds, I get a reward." This kind of rule makes you constantly disappointed. When you do good deeds, do them without any expectation of reciprocity.

This same fallacy of heaven's reward also applies when one "connects conscientiously all the dots," but yet experiences some major setbacks and hence gets depressed. This kind of a person may get a higher education, work long hours, pay mortgage payments on time, chauffeur children to hobbies and so forth, but life offers, for instance, a serious illness. With an expectation of heaven's reward, that kind of outcome seems infeasible, and this big discrepancy leads to depression. If you suffer from a fallacy of heaven's reward, ask yourself: "Am I doing everything for an ulterior motive? Am I perhaps seeking acceptance? Am I simply copying what other people seem to be doing?"

2.2 Four thought pattern families

From the collection of sixteen distorted thought patterns described above, it is easy to recognize overlaps. Hence a completely new collection was created for this book by building distorted thought pattern "families" from the distorted thought patterns. The original collection is, however, important because it shows all the different nuances.

This combination process generated only four distorted thought pattern families. A small collection like this could be called a straightforward, "nuanceless" everyday collection, because this limited number of thought pattern families is already easy to keep in mind in that everyday life, where sweat is trickling down the spine and certain words, which may later cause regret, come easily out of your mouth. In that kind of situation, the first thing in your mind is not to ponder if you are magnifying, labeling, or overgeneralizing.

Before we proceed to the compact collection of thought pattern families, I would like to remind you that it is possible also for you, as your own life's researcher, to work up existing knowledge, instead of just only following instructions blindly (or alternatively resisting everything and never following any instructions). For one of my goals is to awaken you to act and to take power of your own life by yourself. At the same time, you are taking responsibility. Finally, when you have enough strength, you can start to take care of other people and your environment.

The relationship of the four thought pattern families to the sixteen thought patterns is as follows:

Four thought pattern families	Collection of sixteen thought patterns
extreme thinking (extremism)	all-or-nothing thinking
	overgeneralization
	mental filter
	disqualifying the positive
	jumping to conclusions
	magnification or minimization
	labeling
fallacy of control	personalization
	blaming
	always being right
	fallacy of change
	fallacy of control
	fallacy of fairness
	fallacy of heaven's reward
emotional reasoning	emotional reasoning
should statements	should statements

1. Extreme thinking

What is the common denominator for all-or-nothing thinking, overgeneralization, having a mental filter, disqualifying the positive, jumping to conclusions, magnification or minimization, and labeling? The common denominator is going to an extreme. Going to the extreme means that on a thought segment, a thought is placed to an extreme end of it or that the thought is allowed to grow disproportionate in size. A breadcrumb grows into a loaf. A fly becomes a Tyrannosaurus. An extremist way to grow the proportions is also represented by the case where one unsuccessful deed covers its doer in entirety.

You understand the placement error of a thought better when you first imagine that a thought is a segment or a line. A balanced, mature person seeks to get to the middle region of that segment. That is where the segment doesn't sway, doesn't tilt, doesn't trip. A person who is depressed or prone to depression hurtles instead to the extreme end of a thought segment in which case the segment tilts askew like a seesaw where the weight is only on one end. That skewed seesaw works like a slippery slope down to depression. A thought escaping to the extreme end of a thought segment is called here *extremism* or *extreme thinking.*

An **all-or-nothing** thought pattern's segment is made of different shades of grey and only the segment ends are either white or black. Shades of gray represent moderation, various options, adequacy as a human being, and recognition of life's imperfectness, but to an all-or-nothing thinker, everything is either perfect or perfectly unsuccessful.

His room of movement is only in the extreme ends of the thought segment, thus he is an extremist thinker. His seesaw gets always skewed, usually with the black end against the gravel.

In **overgeneralization**, everything is literally taken "over." It is extremism to assume that when something happened once in a certain way, in the future, a similar thing happens always in that same certain way. If an overgeneralizer doesn't get into the university on his first attempt, he thinks that it's not worthwhile trying for the second time because he will never get in. Instead of that thought, he should work on a solution about how that second attempt would turn out differently if he otherwise has already shown both talent and enthusiasm towards his chosen field.

A mental filter represents again a segment in which, between black and white, there are life's colors from the violets and blues through greens and yellows to reds. The mental filter is situated in the black end of the segment. Even if some experience would cover all colors, a mental filter makes a person see only black. Let's take literally a multicolor life experience: a picnic with good company in a park on a sunny summer day. Everyone seems to be having fun, the box lunch is delicious, discussions are sometimes profound, sometimes hilarious, and almost everyone wants to fly the kite. What kind of memory was left for the person who saw everything through his mental filter? Unfortunately, he only remembers that slices of tomato and cream cheese dropped from the top of a sandwich and stained his shirt, and he later felt embarrassed walking through the town with a dirty shirt on.

As you learned from above, **disqualifying the positive** is an extreme version of mental filter. Where the mental filter sees only the negative, a disqualifier of the positive sees negative and *in addition* he alters even the positive as a negative. Hence the disqualifier of the positive sits even more tightly on the extreme black end of the colorful segment of life, in the blackest of all blacks. Let's assume that the disqualifier of the positive was also on that same sunny picnic as the mental filter person. How does he look back on that day? He, too, was so unlucky that he stained his shirt, so naturally he remembers that negative experience. In addition, if he is asked, there wasn't enough wind for the kite, seagulls' cries, tram's rattling, and children's voices bothered him, it was too dark and cool in the shadowy spots and too bright and hot in the sunny spots of the park, despite the general praise, the box lunch was not all that special, jokes didn't make him laugh, red wine was cheap and bad-tasting, and no one had anticipated that he would have rather drank cider.

When **jumping to conclusions**, imagination is taken to an extreme end. Naturally that extreme end is negative, the black end of a thought segment. In *mind reading*, negative conclusions, which have no foundation in reality, are drawn of another person. In *the fortune teller error*, wrongful, negative conclusions are drawn of the future. That, too, is extremism that conclusions stemming merely from one's imagination are considered as full truth.

Magnification or minimization, as even their names suggest, refer to an error in proportions. A small thing is exaggerated into a big thing, a big thing is belittled into a small thing. As actions both represent extremism.

As you learned from above, **labeling** represents overgeneralization taken to an extreme. A mistake, even a big one, is still only a mistake. However, in labeling, it traps into itself also the maker of the mistake. The mistake maker, upon making a mistake, is a "loser," a failure, dumb, or an idiot. This is a question of an extreme error in proportions: a mistake is only a raisin; the maker is an ocean-liner. One raisin can't determine an entire ocean-liner.

In addition to human beings, labeling can also be used on events: "World's worst festival!" "History's stupidest passing!"

Unfortunately, a lot of people have been conditioned to extremism, and an excellent teacher for this skill, together with our fellow men, has been the media. Especially the tabloid headlines are extravagant, strangely emphasized, and deliberately misleading. Articles themselves can be full of speculation (jumping to conclusions). Hence we can conclude that extremism sells. This same extremism can also be seen from readers' comments in newspaper articles. Very often these comments succumb to exaggeration (magnification), that is, to a distortion thought pattern, which is most common among anxiety sufferers.

Extremism and immoderation are siblings, and therefore it is interesting that *moderation* is considered as a personality strength and virtue of happy and positive people. One could conclude that it would be wise to try to learn moderation. In everything.

At this point, a visual person may benefit from an image in which the room of movement for all kinds of thoughts is within a big beach ball. On the surface of that ball are the extreme thoughts and in the middle of the ball are the moderate "middle of the road" thoughts. Extreme thoughts that are positive are on the surface in the upper right quarter. There they represent bubbling joy, happiness, and love. The most negative thoughts are on the surface in the lower left quarter. The aim is to learn to navigate within that beach ball in such a way that one remains as much as possible around the center of the ball. In addition, it is nice to visit the happy upper right quarter whenever the situation permits.

If you have a tendency to hurtle to an extreme in your thinking, then the corrective move can as well be easily extreme. Keep that in mind as you proceed in this book. Even in driver's education, it is taught that an inexperienced driver makes easily a corrective move that is too big, and the car swerves from one edge of the road to another. An experienced driver and an experienced thought straightener knows that sometimes it takes only a few notches of controlled move to correct a mistake.

If you have a tendency for extremism, you may also expect to see changes extremely fast. If you don't see immediately that you are changing, you give up, and return to your old ways. Therefore, make a mark into your calendar exactly one year from this day forward. Write a short diary entry today about how you tend to think now and about how you feel. When exactly a year has passed, stop to think how you think differently about things and how you feel. The prerequisite is, of course, that you are changing your thinking little by little into a more positive direction.

2. Fallacy of control

What is the common denominator for personalization, blaming, always being right, a fallacy of change, a fallacy of control, a fallacy of fairness, and a fallacy of heaven's reward? The common denominator is a fallacy of control. It is the fallacy of control when a person thinks he has the right to control other people, even though a person should control only himself. That, too, is the fallacy of control when a person thinks that other people have the right to control him. Hence in all cases, the fallacy of control involves other people or perhaps in the case of the fallacy of heaven's reward — God or the universe. The fallacy of control gives a mental image that the boundaries of a human suffering from this fallacy are gauzy or "pudding-like" and not exact, tight, and healthy. One's boundaries should stop to oneself, but in people suffering from these thought distortions, they expand further out and swallow a different number of other people inside of them. Alternatively, one's boundaries can shrink inwards, which allows other people to invade the area that ought to be controlled by one self alone. If the boundaries stop to oneself in a healthy way and are "skin-tight," a person carries responsibility and is better aware of his own contribution to both his own misfortune and fortune.

In **personalization**, boundaries of control extend and cover at least the nearest and dearest. When these close ones don't act as expected or don't do all that well in life, the sufferer of this thought distortion feels guilty. There is also similar gauziness or "pudding-likeness" in one's boundaries of control when a person thinks that he is the talk of the town. A person with tight and healthy boundaries doesn't get all that worried even if others do talk about him. A person with tight and healthy boundaries knows that only his own thoughts affect him and then the insinuations of others don't matter.

In **blaming**, a person has enclosed within his boundaries other people whom he can blame when his own life is not going well. Thereby a blamer suffers from the fallacy of control.

When a person thinks he **is always right**, he wants to control other people by being the leader in every situation, having that very last word. It is the fallacy of control to fantasize that one could have a permission to control others by determining autocratically about the truth.

The **fallacy of change** is the fallacy of control. One's own boundaries are not tight, but instead they spread like a pudding around other people. A person suffering from the fallacy of change tries to control others by alternately praising and pressuring, so he himself could be happier. Pressuring may be a mild expression to those who have experienced this kind of pressure, for example, from a narcissistic spouse. In reality, pressuring can involve public humiliation, insults, threats, blackmail, and outright violence.

The **fallacy of control** thought pattern gives its name to the entire family of the fallacy of control. In this case, the control may extend to include other people, as above, but it may also shrink. That is to say that the pudding may spread widely, but it may also shrink into a droplet. While a healthy person's boundaries of control run along his surface, in a shrunk state a person assumes that others have the right to invade his own territory and that is as it should be. A person leaves himself completely to the mercy of others and plays the second fiddle in his own philharmonic.

In the **fallacy of fairness**, a person wants to control other people with his own sense of fairness. His sense of fairness is his personal standpoint, and everyone has to have that same standpoint.

In the **fallacy of heaven's reward** presumably God or the universe is included within the boundaries of one's control. Because who else keeps score of good deeds, noble self-denial, or "conscientiously connecting all the dots?"

Should statements and **emotional reasoning** are the only distorted thought patterns that form alone a respective thought pattern family.

In the everyday hustle and bustle, this kind of "nuanceless" collection of only four distorted thought pattern families is already easy to keep in mind.

When your emotions are stirred up, you get quick help simply by asking yourself: "Did I go to the extreme in my interpretations?" "Did I distort the proportions?" If your answer is "yes," you know you fell into a trap of extreme thinking. You get out of your trap by moving towards the center of the thought segment, towards moderation. Often a small corrective move is sufficient. Remember, if you are an extreme thinker, your corrective move may also easily be extreme.

When your emotions are stirred up, ask also yourself: "What is my share in this matter?" "Did I step on someone else's territory?" "Did I allow other people invade my territory?" "Am I trying to change this other person?" "Am I sticking my nose to something, which is really none of my business?" With these kinds of questions, you can find out if you got tangled up in a fallacy of control. Learn to distinguish between caring and controlling if your role involves taking responsibility for other people. You may influence, but you can't control. You may demand and expect good behavior and conduct, but you can't control whom the other people truly are deep down.

By reducing the distorted thought patterns to only four basic families has yet another benefit. At the same time as the thought patterns are reduced to families, they reveal the forest from the trees. They expand to cover also behavior, corrective moves, ways to react and interpret having those same common denominators, extremism or a fallacy of control in the background. For instance, in behavior, it is possible to go to extreme in working, cleanliness, hoarding, eating, drinking, saving, spending, gambling, and so forth. When it comes to corrective moves, often a subtle move would be completely sufficient, but an extremist goes easily to another extreme end. Let's assume, for instance, that in the childhood home, a child's parents maintained nearly a military standard of order and cleanliness, but instead, after becoming an adult, the same child would loosen up on the cleanliness of his own home, he ends living in the middle of insanitary chaos and dirt.

The fallacy of control, that is to say, invading to other people's territories or allowing other people to invade to one's own territory will be discussed again in Chapter Five of this book. As it turned out, an exactly similar kind of fallacy of control surfaced also in the context of maturation into an authentic adult.

You may already admit that distorted thoughts influence your mood. Next you may wonder why you think such thoughts. The reason is that distorted thoughts feel like real and truthful thoughts.

In traditional psychotherapy, the emphasis has been on emotions. The aim is that a person becomes aware of his own feelings and expresses them more openly. It is thought that the ability to express one's feelings is a sign of emotional maturity. In cognitive psychotherapy, emphasis is on thoughts. It would seem apparent that one should focus on thoughts because thoughts determine the feelings. In addition, a person is able to learn to work on his thoughts. On the other hand, an evolved and mature human being dares to express his feelings, so emotions and their expression shouldn't be ignored either.

For reasons of clarity, cognitive psychotherapy does not, by any means, deny feelings. Feelings can exist from sadness to joy and the other way around. Reasonable feelings of anger are also perfectly normal. Cognitive psychotherapy only wants to get rid of the distorted emotions, and those result from distorted thoughts. Those are the feelings you, as well, want to get rid of, and your request is being answered.

EXTREME
THINKING

FALLACY OF
CONTROL

"SHOULD"
STATEMENTS

EMOTIONAL
REASONING

3 Silent assumptions

When you straighten your distorted thought patterns, your mood gets better. If you had to start the straightening work from a level of depression, your mood improvement can lead to a recovery from depression. It feels like a dark, impenetrable thicket is little by little turning into an open, passable meadow. In the meadow, things look as they truly are: mere problems having solutions to them or if they are not solvable, you have a new attitude towards them.

A change in thinking can sometimes be so big that a person has difficulties to even believe afterwards how he could have thought in such a distorted way — how he could have willfully run himself into that dark thicket. When everything seems bright again, it is hard to believe that one could end up in that dark thicket *again*. However, that can happen even to a person who already knows the distortions of his thinking and won't fall a victim to them. Why? Because the work is not quite done yet. Thought distortions have been straightened, but silent assumptions are still lurking in the background. They, too, need to be addressed. Silent assumptions form a key for the *prevention* of depression.

Silent assumptions color how you see yourself, other people, this life, and the world. Silent assumptions are beliefs. With silent assumptions, you specify your own worth. You already learned from *1.2 Self-worth and self-esteem* about your immeasurable worth, but in some situations, you may still think differently. A silent assumption is silent, because you don't necessarily consciously think what you consider being true in this life. However, it is what you believe in quietly that once again affects "absolutely everything" — it affects your thoughts, speech, humor, choices, behavior, maturity, satisfaction, and happiness. Silent assumptions can, for instance, reveal themselves in thoughts like these: "My life is ruined if I don't get married." "They can't do without me at work. If I'm gone for more than two days, the whole firm is in disarray." "No one makes it in this country because authorities are building these barriers." "I will get more appreciation after I get my Ph.D." "The one with most money has the most worth as a human being."

If you have distorted silent assumptions, you predispose yourself to depression or at least to unpleasant feelings. It is time to examine how truthful these silent assumptions are. There are different kinds of silent assumptions, and every person has a unique collection of them. Some of the silent assumptions are, however, universal and only those can be discussed here.

3.1 Approval

Are you worried what other people think of you? If you answered "yes," it may be that you are way too dependent on others because you rate yourself through other people's eyes. Other people have such a strong influence on you that you automatically depreciate yourself if someone offends or criticizes you. Because the approval from other people is so important to you, they can easily take advantage of you and lead you on.

When someone criticizes or disapproves of you, you believe his words without question, and your mood collapses. When someone praises you, you purr like a cat and for a moment you are happy. In other words, you swallow pretty much without chewing all the criticism and praise. This means that you make other people way too important and believe that they are right. You operate only as an amplifier, and other people's thoughts become directly *your* thoughts. You have already learned from this book that it is only your own thoughts that affect your mood.

Has it ever occurred to you that when someone disapproves of you, the disapprover himself may have a problem? The disapprover may have a bad day, he is envious of you, socially immature, has low self-worth, has distorted thought patterns, or distorted silent assumptions.

What if you made an honest mistake and there is a reason to disapprove of you? In such a case, keep in mind, once again, that there is no equal sign between a deed and a doer. In the same manner, there is no equal sign between approval from others and one's own self-worth. These kinds of equations are wrong in the mathematics of life.

It is, of course, human and understandable that approval makes one feel good and disapproval stings. The question is how deep one swims. Swimming is taken too deep, if approval and disapproval are linked to a perception of self-worth.

The reason why you developed an addiction to approval may be hidden in your childhood and in the relationships of that time. Your parents or other close people may have been unreasonably strict when you didn't behave well. They may have been irritated also when you didn't do anything wrong. Maybe you had to listen to that you are naughty or mean or bad, or you had to listen to that you always end up goofing up. As a little child, you probably saw your parents almost god-like. They knew everything, they taught you to walk, talk, and tie your shoelaces. For most part, prohibitions were literally true, like, for instance, when your mother shouted that you would die if you run across a road without looking. This way you learned to assume that almost everything your parents said was true. Then when you heard that you are naughty, or you were told that you never learn anything, you believed it to be literally true and it hurt. You were too young to reason that your mother or father fell into a trap of extremism that made her or him magnify or overgeneralize. You weren't also mature enough to notice that your mother or father was irritated or tired or hung-over that day and only wanted some peace and quiet. So the question was more of your mother or father's problem, and you only happened to be in the wrong place at the wrong time. If, at an older age, you already learned to notice that your mother or father wrestled with her or his own problems, and you snapped back something relating to that, you may have been quickly restored to old ways with shouting and detention. It was as if your operating system was reverted from a more advanced version back to an old version: yes, mother and father are right.

It is then no wonder that you developed a habit that makes you automatically depreciate yourself every time you receive criticism or even some innocent guidance. It was not your fault that you picked up this habit as a child, because you were unintentionally programmed towards that direction. Now at an older age, you are, however, responsible that you think about this and learn to leave this vulnerability behind you. This vulnerability is based on a fear of disapproval and predisposes you to anxiety and depression.

When you update your silent assumption on approval, you become independent, and you have a healthy idea of your self-worth. Then when you receive criticism or disapproval, your self-worth doesn't sink anymore. You are also able to keep a deed and a doer separate from each other. If your deed deserves criticism, you correct your mistake. You also learn to notice when a disapprover's motives lie in his own low self-worth. Those kinds of comments you know to leave alone. It is also possible for you to avoid company in which you constantly receive mere slander. There are over seven billion people in this world from whom you can choose much better company for yourself.

3.2 Love

Do you think that there is no way you can be happy unless you have a beloved? If your answer is "yes" and you are willing to make significant concessions only to be in a relationship, you may be "a love addict." Then you measure your worth based on the fact whether or not someone loves you. Your silent assumption can take the following form: "Without a beloved I am nothing."

The fact that one hopes to be loved and in a relationship is obviously not wrong. It only becomes unhealthy if being in a relationship is so important to you that it affects your self-worth and happiness. Because you measure your worth with a relationship, you may be subservient and clingy in order to keep your relationship, because otherwise you are afraid you'll drive your partner away. The end result is often, however, that your worst fear realizes when you beloved loses respect for you and feels that you are a burden. When you notice that you are starting to drift apart, you experience withdrawal symptoms. Then you act like any other drug addict — you bulldoze, extort, manipulate, bribe, cry, fawn on, suck up, shout, sulk, beg, make promises, and so on. It is likely that your behavior will drive your beloved away once and for all.

Dependence on love goes often hand in hand with the above-described desire for approval. Then you think that you have to earn love and in order to get yourself a beloved you must do exactly as he wants you to do.

You may also have a distorted belief that if you are independent, you would be considered as cold and stand-offish and then at least you would end up alone. If this is your fear, you have drawn an equal sign between *dependency* and *good-heartedness*. This, again, is a wrong kind of equation in the mathematics of life. Greater independence means only that you are happy also then when you are by yourself. When you are independent, you have several interests, and you don't constantly think only about forming a relationship or maintaining one. The more independent you are, the more certain you can be about your feelings. Then you are able to choose your beloved truly out of love.

Alternatively, you may have a belief that you are entitled to receive from others what you want and when you want. If you don't have a beloved, then you think that you have been treacherously deprived of your entitlement to love, which automatically belongs to you. You are then angry, hungry, and bitter. This kind of attitude drives you more and more isolated.

It is also a totally unreasonable demand that loving you should be left solely as your beloved's work project. No one manages to constantly declare his or her love to another. In fact, your loving you is primarily your own work project. You yourself make an authentic and constantly bubbling source of love for you. You did remember to tell yourself also this morning that you love yourself, didn't you?

Keep also in mind that there is a big difference between a need and a want. Oxygen, which we breathe, is a need. Love is a want. It is *extremism* to describe a want for love as a need for love, that is, as a necessity for life. If you describe love as a need, you "easily sell yourself short." That "short" is represented, for instance, by wrong kinds of compromises, subservience, and ignoring clear warning signs in a selection of a spouse.

3.3 Achievement

Do you think that a person has to be useful and productive or otherwise his life is meaningless? Do achievements and success increase a person's worth? If a person fails in his work-life, has he then failed as a human being? In Western societies quite a few answer "yes" to these questions and perhaps you belong to that same group.

If your worth as a human being is based on achievement and success, your idea of humanity is restricted. You see yourself as a commodity. If you go on a vacation or earnings of your business take a plunge or you retire or you get ill and are no longer able to work, you are in danger of collapsing mentally.

It has to be stated immediately and more precisely under this silent assumption that there is absolutely nothing wrong per se that a person is productive and successful. On the contrary, productivity and success will bring satisfaction and enrichment for life. A whole lot of successful people have improved tremendously this world with their inventions, creativity, and entertainment. The love and passion of many of these successful people towards their work is admirable. That, too, is true that financial success increases happiness to a certain point. A problem is generated only when one builds a connection between one's self-worth and success, achievement, certificates, and job titles. This kind of link is destructive, erroneous, and malignant. This distorted silent assumption can be summed up as follows: "My worth as a human being is directly proportional to what I accomplish in my life."

This performance-requiring silent assumption is likely to motivate you to produce on a high level. You may put extra effort on your career because you are convinced that this is the way to collect extra bonuses on self-worth and with a big bonus balance you are a more eligible human being in other people's eyes.

What is on the other side of the coin? If your business is successful or your career is progressing, you may enslave yourself from dawn to dusk so that you inadvertently detach yourself from other joys and pleasures of life. As your "workaholism" gets worse, you have a greater need to be productive, because if you fail to keep up your hard pace at work, you will feel severe withdrawal symptoms. They feel as internal emptiness and despair. When you don't get new achievements, you feel unworthy.

What happens, if due to an illness, recession, bankruptcy, retirement, or for some other reason you will not be able to perform on a level you are used to? Then you may sink into depression because you think you are of less value. If due to your business or work career you neglected your family that, too, may bring its own punishment. Your family may have endured the situation for a long time, but eventually your spouse may leave or betray you, and your children may get into a variety of difficulties. Alternatively, due to your high drive for high performance, you never even had a chance to start a family even if you wanted to. No matter how it all played out, you are left with one big detriment: lack of authentic self-worth.

Just like in any addiction, you notice that you need increasingly bigger doses of the drug you are using. Your tolerance increases with respect to the pursuit of property, fame, and success. Why? Because you automatically lift your expectations higher after you have reached the previous level.

Performance, achievement, and all kinds of success are, after all, only deeds. You have already learned that you should never place an equal sign between a deed and a doer even though a whole lot of people do so. So do also the workaholics and those who yearn for fine titles.

The nature of a deed needs to be opened up here more. For starters, a deed is very limited, time-wise. It is a single small dot on a long segment of one's life. When you attach your worth to your deeds, you are on cloud nine when you hit a success point. Life, however, doesn't stop at a single point, but continues. That is to say, you can't park on a success point for the rest of your life. If there isn't a new success point shortly after the previous one, you collapse on the base line and that feels awful. It feels totally mediocre.

Many successful people may have a straight line of success points without any gaps. They don't need to step on the baseline, because they simply hop from one success point to another. For instance, for a young scientist, his first success point is an important finding in his research. Next in line is the first scientific article in an international scientific publication, then a second one, soon a doctoral thesis, and so forth. Decades of career years can swish past in a good hum. It is often so that a person successful in his career stops only in his more mature age to ask, if this is all there is. Why am I melancholic, even though everything is so incredibly well?

It is even unhappier for those who face an unexpected setback. Grants are exhausted, the company reorganizes and ends employment, or one's own business goes bankrupt due to a global economic situation. This kind of situation is horrific to a person whose self-worth is linked to striving and titles. Out with employment or a business goes also one's self-worth. Embarrassment and shame follow. Desperation is sometimes so great that the route out is self-destruction.

Are all successful people prisoners of this distorted silent assumption? Of course not. A part of successful people doesn't simply link their success to their self-worth. They are working hard purely out of love and passion and in addition they are successful. More prone to depression are those who have chosen their own field mainly on the grounds that that field is valued and pays well. This choice could be summed up as follows: "When I am in that prestigious field and I earn lot of money, my self-worth increases. Other people admire and respect me. Now I feel inferior, but that notion will improve once I reach my goals."

It is, of course, possible that a field chosen for wrong reasons turns out to be the right one, and vice versa, a field chosen with a heart turns out to be something else than one had imagined. If the choice proves to be wrong, then the best way to get it right is with a flexible attitude, preparedness for changing the job, or even the entire field. It might be possible to modify the current job, so it becomes more workable. A tedious job could possibly be balanced by designing a more interesting leisure time during which one can fulfill one's passions as hobbies. If you consider yourself as being valuable from the get-go, without false external trappings and ornaments, it is easier to be flexible.

If you still believe that success makes a person somehow more special and valuable, think how the majority of people never achieve great success, but yet they are happy. Hence the basis for happiness and love can't be in great success and achievements. In addition, depression doesn't respect social position, thickness of one's wallet, or huge groups of fans, but it can strike in humble dwellings as well as in big mansions. That is to say that success and achievement do not protect from depression.

If you still think that the benefits of this silent assumption outweigh the disadvantages, ask yourself with your hand on your heart: "Will I love and respect myself even if I endure a significant failure?"

3.4 Perfectionism

"If you are not able to do something well, it is not worthwhile doing at all." Is this one of your favorite phrases? Do you also think that it is shameful to show weakness? Is it your guideline that a person must try to be the best in everything he undertakes? Do you get upset, if you make a mistake? Are you afraid that you will end up a second-class citizen if you don't set the highest standards for yourself? If you answered "yes" to previous questions, you are a perfectionist. Like all the silent assumptions presented here, also this fourth assumption often leads to anxiety and depression.

As a perfectionist you demand a lot from yourself and others. In your world, mistakes, failures, and even negative feelings are forbidden. Usually your perfectionism doesn't limit to your undertakings, but you believe that you should feel great, behave greatly, look great, and think great thoughts all the time. You demand positive thoughts from yourself, but in reality you are often frustrated because everything is somehow incomplete, imperfect. When you reach a target, the next goal is already looming in the horizon, and eventually you wonder why the promised rewards don't seem to materialize. You think that you are just not good enough. In reality you are really good, but your expectations are unreasonably high.

Did you know that perfection does not even exist? Everything can be improved if one looks at it close enough and judgmentally. Thus it is worthwhile proportioning one's expectations to that authentic imperfection surrounding us, not to imaginary perfection.

At least the pursuit of perfection has one benefit: it protects you from failure, from being exposed to criticism, and from disapproval. A real tragedy arises when a student is talented, a perfectionist, and always manages to keep failures at bay. Naturally, he also completes his studies with best grades. Continued success may convert these kinds of students into cripples and slaves because they are desperately trying to drive off failing. Their careers may be successful, but often the joy in life and work is meager. You may have never thought about your pursuit of perfection from this point of view.

What are you then afraid of? Your fear is that if you fail, you are seen as a failure. It is important to you what other people think of you, but because the only thing that affects your mood is what you yourself think, then your biggest fear is this: you yourself would think you are a failure. A deed and a doer is the same thing to you. You have already learned that link is totally wrong.

If you would implement moderation and balance in your life, then you would set yourself flexible challenges, which are of correct and proper size. You would feel satisfaction from the making and doing itself, and you would not solely examine the end result. It is a great relief when you don't need to be excellent in everything and try to do your best all the time. There is no reason to be afraid of making mistakes, because we always learn something new from making them. A more relaxed way also makes a person more productive and creative.

A severe form for the pursuit of perfection is the obsessive-compulsive pursuit of perfection. That is when a person focuses on details, feels compulsion to finish everything at once, and demands a strict order. Because of his obsessive-compulsive pursuit of perfection, a person may be slow or even unable to do anything because all the details make the whole look huge and therefore overwhelming.

On the other end of the spectrum for the pursuit of perfection are perfectionists who have "only" high standards. Psychologist *Joachim Stoeber's* study shows that there are three different types of these high standard perfectionists. In the first group are those who set high standards *for themselves*. In the second group are those who believe that *other people* expect perfection from them. In the third group are those who require high standards *from others*.

First group members, who expect perfection from themselves, can be distinguished from the other two groups based on the humor they cultivate. Their humor is benevolent, positive, and self-accepting.

Perfectionists that belong to the second group try to be perfect because they assume that people close to them, at school, at a study- or at a work-place expect perfect performance. Members of this group have low self-worth. Their means for getting approval is through a pursuit of perfection. Their way to seek approval shows also in their humor. In their jokes, they often make fun at their own expense, depreciating themselves.

The third group of perfectionists sets unreasonable demands on others. Members of this group feel superiority towards other people and their sense of humor is aggressive. They also joke at other people's expense.

A perfectionist may express strongly all three types of the above-described groups or only one or two of them.

The fact that a person sets high standards for himself doesn't necessarily cause significant psychological problems, except in a case of eating disorders. These self-imposed high standards help a person succeed. This kind of pursuit of perfection is not a problem if the perfectionist himself thinks that his tendency to perfection doesn't cause any harm, but is a pure benefit and pleasure.

The fact that a person feels that other people require perfection from him, may, instead, lead to anxiety and depression.

The fact that a person demands perfection from other people leads to constant state of anger. Over time, that constant state of anger may also be a slope leading down to depression. Belonging to this third group may also be a sign of a serious personality disorder, such as narcissism.

If you consider yourself as a perfectionist, ask yourself if this is causing problems to you or others. Is it driving you to depression? Does it make you anxious? Does the pursuit of perfection lower your life satisfaction? Does it affect your relationships? Are you constantly irritated because of it? If your answer is "no," you may keep your pursuit of perfection at the level it is, since it is also a positive force and helps you succeed.

Perfectionists are usually advised to lower their requirements. This kind of lowering of standards *across the board* may be the right answer to an obsessive-compulsive perfectionist, but to several other perfectionists a better solution might be to lower requirements in *part* of the performance. Even requirements can have prioritization applied to them, which means setting different activities in an order of importance. Some things should still be done at one hundred percent accuracy, for some others as little as a 60 percent grade is sufficient. All of us want that a brain surgeon works at one hundred percent accuracy when he is correcting an aneurysm. Instead, a number of everyday repetitive things should not be done at a one hundred percent level. It is sufficient to have well-washed windows; they don't need not be "perfectly" washed. Therefore, it is worthwhile for a perfectionist to consider what he wants to do conscientiously, and where he can relax his grip a little bit.

Another object of development for a perfectionist is shortening the time he uses in his work. Quite often a slow pace of work emphasizes the tendency for perfection, stumbling on details. Speed does not necessarily mean that the quality suffers. The best brain surgeons are accurate, but at the same time they are expeditious.

While perfection shows itself partially in a gloomy light in here, nonetheless don't be afraid to use the word "perfect" in the future when you describe things, which you don't want to change in the slightest. The fact that you cultivate that word in that context shows how positive and grateful you are for life. "This spring has been really perfect." "I have never tasted anything so perfectly scrumptious!"

3.5 Entitlement

"If I strongly believe I deserve something, I can expect to get it. Of course I get frustrated, if I find obstacles in my way of getting what I want. When I put other people's needs before my own, they should help me when I need something from them. Because I'm a good spouse, my partner has to love me. When I do nice things to others, I can expect that they respect me and treat me just as well as I treat them." Are these preceding sentences in line with your expectations? If they are, your silent assumption is a sense of entitlement. Once again this is an assumption that predisposes to anxiety and depression.

If your sense of entitlement is strong, you feel that you have the right to get success, love, and happiness. You expect and demand that other people and the universe fulfill your desires because you are a good human being and you have worked hard. When things don't work out — as often happens — you choose between two alternatives: you get depressed and feel that you are a failure or you get furious. You are bitter most of the time. You constantly moan, but you do very little to solve your problems. In the end, you feel entitled, so it's the universe and other people's tasks to solve your problems.

A sense of entitlement is based on *controlling others* and *taking away from others*. Then sense of entitlement could be summed up as follows: "I want this and I want it by means of you!" When you have this kind of sense of entitlement, you are not interested in knowing how your wanting affects other people. You just want it and preferably here and now.

In a strong sense of entitlement, the objects for your control and stealing are not necessarily only other people, but the object can also be a society or the universe. You may then fret and fume at the universe: "Life gave me nothing!" At the same time, you forget the abundance, which you are already enjoying, and you think that you yourself don't need to do anything for your desires.

A person who gets easily angry tends to draw up his sense of entitlement and desire in a moral form: "If I'm nice to others, they should be reciprocally nice towards me. They should show their gratitude." If you think that other people behave as you expect them to behave, then you expect that we all are exactly like you. It is worthwhile giving up this kind of sense of entitlement or else you end up staying irritated for the rest of your life.

If one's sense of entitlement is thought to be a segment, on the other extreme end of it is that above-mentioned controlling of others and taking away from others. That is: a sense of entitlement which has extremism, "should" statements, and personalization behind it. On the other extreme end of that same segment is, naturally, a total lack of a sense of entitlement. The sense of entitlement is next to zero. A person feels so worthless that he thinks he is not entitled to anything. What then could be found from the healthy middle region of that segment? That is where there is a benign sense of entitlement, and that is simply *a positive sense of expectation*. That is where a person believes in himself, and he dreams of achieving good things in life. That is where a person knows himself, knows how to dream, and combines the right kind of action to his dreams to get what he wants. In the healthy middle region of the segment, a person has self-confidence, and he knows he can carry out his dreams without a need to steal from others or to control others. Fulfilling one's dreams may include collaboration, but that is not stealing or controlling. On the healthy middle region of the segment, a person doesn't automatically feel entitled, but he asks about things, takes action, and negotiates. In the healthy middle region of the segment, a person knows that other people are unique and different, and he respects that. Thus there is no law of nature why things should always go exactly as he wants them to go. Of course a person, who relates to things in this healthy way, gets disappointed during those occasions when the outcome is not positive, but the disappointment doesn't sink him to the depths of misery. Why not? Because this person is a "percentage player" who doesn't expect full reciprocity or "justice" every single time. He is patient and tenacious, and he has a high tolerance for disappointments. As a result of it he often copes better than others.

This subchapter is finished with a story of a distorted sense of entitlement:

> A man's wife died. This reduced the man to despair. The man tried to convince himself that it was all about his great grief. He even felt some secret pride that through his fall other people would see that it had been the love story of this century. He believed he was the most loyal and romantic husband in the world's history because he devoted the rest of his life in grieving over his wife. In reality the man thought that the evil universe had broken his rule. In his opinion he should have been entitled to a life-long love story. A variety of distortions in this man's thoughts and silent assumptions produced self-pity and ultimately led to alcoholism and depression.

3.6 Omnipotence

Your silent assumption is omnipotence if you think that you are supposed to carry responsibility on how people close to you feel and how they behave. As an omnipotent person you have to try to help everyone in need of help, because you are a good and moral human being. You also believe that you have to please everyone.

An omnipotent person sees himself as a center of his universe. His own boundaries don't stop at himself, but extend further. Within the boundaries of an omnipotent are strongly also those who belong to his close circle, because he has wrongfully mixed up influencing other people with controlling other people. Influencing is healthy, controlling is not, as you already know from the distorted thought patterns.

Hence an omnipotent person suffers from the fallacy of control. At the same time, as an omnipotent person thinks he is omnipotent, in reality the opposite happens — he is anxious and incapable. Very often perfectionism is mixed with omnipotence. Quite possibly an attempt to control had its roots in frustration when the input by members in the close circle did not reach the high standards of the omnipotent. Then the omnipotent took others' tasks to self so they would be done "right." When a means for controlling and manipulation includes also self-sacrifice, we talk about martyrdom. A martyr suffers, feels overwhelmed by his work and responsibilities, and feels helplessness.

A person, who doesn't see himself as omnipotent, doesn't control other people. Instead he sees them as friendly collaborators. He thinks it is normal human behavior that other people may disagree with him and that they don't follow his advice. People enjoy that they are treated as equals and are respected. Hence people often want a non-omnipotent in an influential position even though he himself doesn't lust for power.

3.7 Autonomy

"I believe strongly that my moods are affected by factors that are outside of my control. These include, for example, my past, these current circumstances, uncertainty about the future, people I'm dealing with, 'body chemistry,' hormone cycles, planetary positions, chance, and fate." You will be exposed to anxiety or even depression if you live in a belief that external factors contribute to how you feel. This puts you in an unfavorable position because you can't control factors outside of yourself. In fact, there is a saying that all of your misery comes from the mistaken belief that you are powerless.

When you believe that influences come from outside of you, you are not independent and self-acting. If, instead, you are an independent person, you understand and acknowledge that all of your moods are children of your own thinking. You take responsibility for your feelings because you recognize that ultimately you yourself gave birth to them.

It is positive to seek independence and self-functionality. If something makes you upset, you know that *you* can influence how you feel about that matter. You can find a silver lining to your potential dark cloud. As an independent person, you ponder different options and try to find a solution. As an independent person, you think that you know best who you are at the core and what you should do to get to your goals — to become the most authentic and happiest self.

If you still believe that you are purely a victim of circumstances, perhaps being independent frightens you. Think what is so frightening about it. Carrying responsibility? Do you think that if you yourself don't choose the direction for your life, you will not get blamed if the choice goes awry? If the feeling of worthlessness has previously subjected you to the mercy of others, hopefully you will experience an increase in your worth through reading this book and at the same time it prepares you towards greater independence.

Yet another valuable lesson for independence has already been taught in this book. It is keeping the deed and the doer separate from one another. For as long as one's deeds have been entangled with oneself (the doer), many decisions and choices have felt positively overwhelming. It is easier to be independent when failed deeds remain as failed deeds and don't mean that the doer is somehow a failure. When deeds remain deeds, one can look at them solution-orientated. Then one can search for new knowledge and ask for help in order to remedy the situation, if remedying is at all possible. If the consequences can't be canceled or remedied, one may ponder how to avoid similar situations in the future. All this reasoning is focused on a solution, not in unproductive slander of oneself. At the same time as you ponder solutions keep in mind *Albert Einstein*'s words: "We cannot solve our problems with the same thinking we used when we created them."

3.8 Updating silent assumptions

The above-described silent assumptions are from the Dysfunctional Attitude Scale (DAS), which was developed by *Arlene Weissman* and presented also in *Feeling good* by David D. Burns. Weissman developed DAS after realizing that even though the number of negative, automatic thoughts declines dramatically between periods of depression, self-destructive belief system still remains more or less unchanged during these better times.

There are other silent assumptions as well. One very typical and crippling silent assumption is that problems disappear by themselves. This silent assumption has spread to every level in a society. A tendency to avoid problems is, in fact, the root cause for mental health problems. The more a person is looking for easy ways out of his problems, the deeper he sinks into his own fantasies, sometimes even completely escaping from reality. Already *Carl Jung* suggested that neurosis is always a substitute for a fact that one would in a matter-of-fact way deal with the sufferings of everyday life and take them one by one off the agenda. Today the word neurosis would be replaced with anxiety.

It is immaturity to imagine that life shouldn't involve hardships or that one is the only one who is experiencing them and life is but sunshine for the others. Every person meets problems in his lifetime. The lightest problems are those one starts to tackle and which are not intentionally exaggerated with self-pity, speculation, explanations, accusations, lies, or by a transfer of responsibility.

Avoiding problems is visible even in therapy. People seek therapy in order to get relief and understanding. Many drop out of therapy because they are made to deal with their problems. Therapy is work.

Another silent assumption that could be mentioned is the general assumption that a negative thinker is realistic and a positive thinker is not. It is as though negativity is wearing a robe of intelligence. At the same time, positive people are seen as being unrealistic and simple airheads. You know that this is not true. Already the previous chapter showed that negativity has *always* distortions in it and distortions are imaginary. Imagining, if anything, is a lack of realism.

Some silent assumptions have their basis on distortions, so the solution is to straighten them. Sometimes silent assumptions are outdated, so the solution is to update them. An example of such could be a silent assumption born during childhood circumstances, which then served well — maybe even by saving one's sanity — but which no longer works for an adult. Let's assume that parents always promise their child all kinds of things, but repeatedly break their promises. Promised holidays never become reality, the promised bicycle never gets purchased, and there are always obstacles to get started with that promised baseball hobby. At some point the child finally learns not to trust the promises his parents make. This new realization brings the child relief because he no longer raises his expectations beforehand and then, after getting disappointed, doesn't fall from as high as when he smaller. Finally, this child becomes an adult, gets married, and has children. He has difficulties keeping his jobs, he is jealous of his spouse, but at the same time, however, distant and cold towards her. Finally, the spouse has enough of it and files for a divorce. What happened? This child, who was constantly betrayed by his parents, never updated his silent assumption after becoming adult that he should never trust anyone. Updating an obsolete silent assumption would have eventually taken less energy and time than what its preservation came to cost in the end.

Behind several mental disorders, life entanglements, poor behavior models, and continuing failures, there may, in fact, be an outdated silent assumption. The surrounding reality may have changed a lot since the days when that silent assumption was created for one's comfort and refuge.

Perhaps at this point you think that the link between that constantly betrayed child and the adult incapable of trusting is quite clear after someone is pointing it out like that, but imagine actually being in the eye of that storm, then it is not all that easy to realize the reason for one's own behavior. This is very true. Recognizing one's own behavior becomes easier, when one becomes a researcher of his own life. It is not as difficult as it sounds. It doesn't require any schooling. It only means pausing, collecting data about oneself by reminiscing about the past, a little pondering and analyzing. Anyone can do it at some level, if only one stops to think, undisturbed.

After realization, encountering issues can, of course, be frightening. Even if that child, who was constantly betrayed by his parents, had realized as an adult the reason for his problems, he should have still taken a risk that he trusts other people. In this case, risk-taking would have represented updating that assumption. Even though his own parents weren't trustworthy, he should have tested his new updated notion that some adults are, as it is.

It may also be frightening to accept that one was not as loved by one's parents as one had always assumed. Even if a person made a frightening discovery that perhaps the parents did not have the ability to love their own child, reflection doesn't have to stop there. The chain of thoughts could be continued, for instance, in such a way that one could also update the significance of one's parents in one's life and thereby disconnect the power given to them. That power given to one's parents may manifest itself, for instance, in such a way that the child, even after becoming an adult, seeks constantly his parents' approval in different ways. Would the parents love more after getting promoted to a CEO position? Do their hearts finally open from two graduate degrees?

Researching one's own life could be continued by reflecting what restrained parent's ability to love. Maybe one discovers that there has been a chain of generations in which lovelessness has only generated new lovelessness. This reflection could bring forgiveness — parents did the best they knew how within the limits of their underdeveloped abilities. It was hard for them to give when there was little to give.

A researcher of one's own life could proceed further from this by, for instance, creating an updated silent assumption that it is possible for a person to create himself a new family from like-minded, loving people who are not necessarily related at all. A relationship with one's own parents may or may not persist, but in any case one doesn't need to hold on to them so tightly anymore that in the thirst for their approval one strives oneself breathless. In fact, psychologist *Craig Malkin* even proposes that an adult child should reduce — or completely avoid — keeping in contact with such parents who refuse to see their own share in mistakes and problems, lie and manipulate without conscience, are incapable of empathy, and abuse mentally or physically. Parents who behave this way suffer from a personality disorder, usually from psychopathy or narcissism. These personality disorders are discussed in more detail in Chapter Five.

If lovelessness has already been handed down from one generation to another, how can it all of a sudden end? Where does the chain breaker get the love he can share in the future? I firmly believe that a person can help himself with this. Even reflecting on the matter — through awareness — is a huge leap on the path towards love. Advancing in growth and maturity brings better health to one's mind and love to one's heart. In the background, there also has to be an unwavering confidence that one's own worth is immeasurable. Everyone can fully and freely choose this concept of one's own immeasurable worth. It doesn't need to be earned, applied for separately, or expected from the outside. It doesn't need to be waited for even timewise, but can be chosen here immediately, if you didn't already dare to do so during reading the first chapter.

3.9 Other silent assumptions

I call those above-described silent assumptions psychological silent assumptions. We can also have cultural and social silent assumptions, which create obstacles in our life. For example, the reasoning in the beginning of this book about scarcity represented one silent assumption. A human being can see the surrounding world as scarce and thus restrictive or abundant and thus enabling.

Silent assumptions have a huge impact in people's lives. Silent assumptions possess power that may completely change the direction of one's life. One's own silent assumptions either enable wonderful things to one's life or they create unnecessary, crippling obstacles. We create some of the obstacles ourselves and some we absorb from our surrounding. In some cultures, swimming in a hole in the ice leads to mortal illness, in others, it gives vitality and improves the immune system. In some cultures, a mother who has recently given birth is not allowed to get out of bed for an entire month — not even allowed to go and take a shower — yet in other cultures the attitude is completely opposite: giving birth is not an illness and very soon after giving birth mothers get out of their beds. People adapt to silent assumptions of their own culture and often operate accordingly and without questioning them.

You could now ponder what kind of silent assumptions you have used to build obstacles into your own life. The fact that other people around you act in a certain way doesn't mean that that way is correct or that it is suitable for you. Ask yourself also this one big question: "Is this world a hostile place where I have to fight to survive or is there goodness and willingness for cooperation in this world if only I reached out to look for it?" Even your notion of this world constitutes one silent assumption on the basis of which you make a lot of choices in your life. Are you absolutely sure that your silent assumption is the correct one? If you altered your assumption, what would that enable for you?

Think what kinds of cultural silent assumptions prevent or complicate your life. Could it be a high time to give them up or at least alter them? Prevailing cultural silent assumptions can be recognized, for instance, from proverbs and idioms. Examples of them have been collected in the table below. Naturally there are also a great number proverbs, quotes, and idioms with deep wisdom in them.

Silent assumption	Rationalization
The fox that sleeps in the morning has not his tongue feathered.	Know thyself! Maybe you belong to a group that is most prolific in the evening or night.
Time heals all wounds.	Time heals only if time is used for healing (for instance, in grieving).
The apple doesn't fall far from the tree. (That is, a child resembles his parents either in good or evil or both).	The apple may fall far or stay close. In many families apples have fallen far when children have boldly looked for their own paths.

Silent assumption	Rationalization
Money doesn't grow on trees. What comes singing, leaves whistling. If hard work was so wonderful, the rich would keep it all for themselves.	Among other things, these phrases suggest that one has to drudge for one's money. However, many people get their income by doing what they love to do. If one's silent assumption is such that the only way to put bread on the table is through slaving away, then that kind of person usually ends up slaving away.
A drop doesn't kill and one can't drown in a bucket. Joy without spirits is pretentious.	An alcoholic or a person becoming one is trying to sanctify his drinking.
You can't teach an old dog new tricks.	This is an excuse when a person is afraid of change. Fortunately, many have already discovered their lifelong ability to learn. Today, schools have students of all ages.
Speech is silver, but silence is golden. You will be named after a wise man, if you keep your mouth shut. Still waters run deep. Empty vessels make most noise.	These proverbs reveal a silent cultural assumption in which an equal sign is put between silence/speechlessness and intelligence. In reality, there are unintelligent quiet ones, intelligent quiet ones, unintelligent loquacious ones, and intelligent loquacious ones. Sure it is recommended that one always thinks first before speaking.

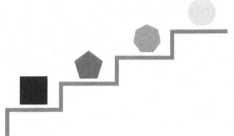

4 Methods for straightening distortions

It would be worthwhile getting rid of distorted thought patterns and silent assumptions, but how? In fact, you have already taken the first step on that path. The fact that you are aware of the existence of these thought patterns and silent assumptions is that very first step, and that step is not short. Previously you didn't recognize them, because you considered your thoughts being fully automatic. This is definitely already progress. Recognition is the first step.

Cognitive psychotherapy is very practical. Its methods for straightening distortions are strikingly simple, but they have been shown to work over the decades. Since you are your own life's researcher, you can also alter the existing methods. It may be the easiest for you to write down your thoughts on a piece of paper or on a text editor page, but if you think writing is appalling, you might as well carry out your chosen methods in your mind. You know which way works best for you.

It is recommended that you modify your thoughts daily. Remember where you started. You may have lived for years, if not even for decades, in a tight squeeze of these distorted thought patterns, and silent assumptions. Hence a mere reading will not guarantee a healed mind — or at least it doesn't guarantee it for a long time.

Most of the methods presented here have been taken from the book *Feeling good* by David D. Burns. In *Feeling good*, methods were presented in the context of problems. Although the problems differed from each other, the methods were still very similar or at least they had some common denominator upon which I could build a basic formula for a method. Thus I ended up reversing the situation: the method itself became the object for presentation. During the presentation of a method, there are suggestions for its use for different problems. From those application examples, you will, at the same time, learn more about distorted thoughts and silent assumptions. Because the design was reversed, the methods also received new names.

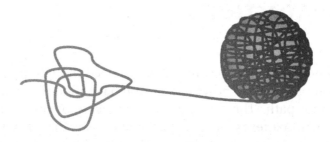

4.1 The most important basic method

This effective and very simple method has only two steps.
1. Learn to recognize a distorted thought pattern or silent assumption.
2. Straighten the distortion with a rational counterargument.

While you ponder your rational counterargument to your distortion, you learn to be realistic, unbiased, and detached.

Remember that the object of recognition is a distorted *thought* and not a *feeling* because it is impossible to find a rational counterargument to a feeling. For instance, "I feel really lousy" doesn't represent a thought. You can't come up with a counterargument to that.

Let's assume your tooth starts to ache. A thought may then automatically flash in your mind: "How stupid can I be! I should have gone to a dentist already six months ago." Alternatively, you may think: "This can only happen to me that a toothache strikes right before the weekend." These are already thoughts and can be addressed with a counterargument like: "It would have been nice if I had remembered to order a dentist's appointment six months ago, but I'm not stupid and no one could have been able to predict that the consequences are immediately this serious" or "For sure I am not the only one who has had this happen right before the weekend."

In the middle of everyday hustle and bustle, it is often enough, if you ask yourself: "Did I immediately jump to the extreme?" If you answered "yes," you get your counterargument when you descend from your extremist interpretation to moderation, to around the middle region of a thought segment. That is where the truth is.

In the middle of everyday hustle and bustle you can also reveal your fallacy of control by asking: "Did I exceed my powers?" "Did I step on someone else's territory?" "Did I give my power away to someone else?"

The idea is that you keep doing this strict and rigorous examination of your thoughts on a daily basis for a few months. This is how the old patterns get broken. If you want to, you can follow how your old patterns are breaking by taking a depression test periodically.

The best way this most powerful basic method can be opened up is through some examples.

Upsetting thought: I always do everything wrong! (Extremism in a form of overgeneralization).
Rational counterargument: I do lot of things right. There is no reason to overgeneralize that I supposedly do *everything* and *always* wrong.

Upsetting thought: I feel wretched to miss the festival, but I'm too tired to do any travelling. I can't enjoy anything in this miserable state of my mind. (Emotional reasoning and extremism in a form of the fortune teller error).
Rational counterargument: The fact that I am now feeling miserable doesn't mean that the festival is miserable. I can't know in advance how I feel once I get there.

Upsetting thought: Today was a lousy day! (Extremism in a form of all-or-nothing thinking).

Rational counterargument: A couple of unpleasant things happened today, that's all. A day like this is still far from a catastrophe.

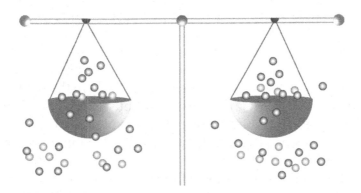

4.2 Weighing method

In a weighing method, matters are put on opposite scales, and they are compared with each other. The weighing method has two steps.

1. Express a claim or a benefit or a rule.
2. Find a counterargument or a disadvantage or a changed rule.

If you have a habit of coming up with excuses that allow you to postpone your work, a weighing method is practical. Tasks that wait to be carried out and problems related to them are your claims. A counterargument is the reason why it is worthwhile for you to take action. As you progress through your claim-counterclaim chain all the way to the end, it is very likely that you're ready to get to work.

You may also use a weighing method if you feel that your work has no value. For instance, you may think: "Anyone could wash these floors." In this case the self-accepting counterargument could sound like this: "Because this is a routine job, I earn extra praise for doing it." Give yourself praise also for other things you have done during the day. This will help you to direct your attention to work that you have already done instead of fretting constantly about things that you haven't done yet.

If you condemn yourself already in advance that you will fail, then a weighing method is excellent. You may insist in your mind: "I never get the basement storage sorted out and year after year more junk just keeps accumulating." Encourage yourself, for example, with this kind of counterargument: "I'll do just a small portion at a time. Maybe I will divide the job to take about half a year."

A weighing method is helpful also in harsh self-criticism. For example, an unemployed, depressed person may insist to himself that he only knows how to lie in bed. In reality, during depression, no one is his own authentic self. This reminder is that counterargument.

A weighing method is also used for reducing moralistic should statements. In this case, should statements are the claims that are questioned by counterarguments. In this way, the irrationality of should statements is revealed.

With a weighing method, you can weigh pros and cons when you have a recurring theme in your life that makes you furious. Consider both short- and long-term consequences.

Benefits for my anger: My anger feels good because then my spouse realizes how much I resent him/her. Even if I don't get what I want at least I get satisfaction from my revenge. I manage to get my spouse to feel the same displeasure I feel. Besides, my spouse behaves always better after I have exploded.

Disadvantages for my anger: I'm turning our bad relationship worse. I often feel guilty after I've exploded. When we are angry, we never deal with the problems themselves. Because of my anger, I'm seen as bad-tempered, capricious, spoiled, erratic, and immature. I may lose my relationship with my children. Maybe as adults, they don't want to have anything to do with me. My spouse will leave me when he/she gets enough of my nagging and tantrums. I feel constantly miserable.

It is worthwhile to continue by making a list of possible positive consequences, if one let's go of the anger. For example, like this:

> My behavior is more predictable. I handle my emotions better. I am more relaxed. People like me more and seek my company. I behave more like an authentic adult. I will get my way better by a convincing, factual, and well-founded negotiation than by bickering and demanding. My spouse, my children, and my parents will respect me more.

With a weighing method, you may also weigh the advantages and disadvantages of your silent assumption. Let's assume, for instance, that you are often requested to take positions of trust. You are flattered, but at the same time you know you are already overworked. You don't dare to refuse, however, because you seek approval. When you weigh the situation, it may turn out that the disadvantages outweigh the advantages.

> *Advantages for accepting positions of trust:* I feel that I master the business when I fulfill people's expectations. I avoid a lot of guilt and confusion when I conform to pleas. I don't need not be worried that people get angry at me or that they despise me.
> *Disadvantages for accepting positions of trust:* I often do things I really don't want to do and which are not beneficial to me. Because of my silent assumption, I never know if people like me the way I truly am. I have to earn approval by doing what other people want me to do. This means I give them too much power. When I rarely make other people unhappy, I feel guilty and depressed. So I let other people control my moods as well! At the same time, however, I feel that other people are so weak and fragile that they are dependent on me. They would be totally lost and unhappy if I disappointed them with a refusal. At this rate, I never have time to pursue my own dreams. I, too, have a dream or two.

A weighing method helps also perfectionists. Let's say that you are a writer, fine artist, composer, or a dancer and you want to create a "perfect" piece of art. In this case, weighing advantages and disadvantages might look like this:

> *Advantages of perfectionism:* I will try to create an extraordinary end result via perfectionism.
> *Disadvantages of perfectionism*: The pursuit of perfection makes me so tight and tense that I am unable to produce high-quality work. I don't want to take the risk that I would fail. Since I'm never perfect, I criticize myself severely, and I'm constantly depressed. Pursuing perfection makes me unbearable in the eyes of others. I point out my friends' faults to them so they, too, would step their game up. I am soon left without any friends because people don't like being constantly judged. I'm so afraid of making mistakes that I only do the old and familiar things, which I'm already good at. At the same time, I'm bored because I don't have any new challenges.

After such weighing you are more open to a change. You dare to try a more relaxed approach on your creative work and you might surprise yourself.

With a weighing method, you may weigh a dysfunctional rule and deliberate whether you want to modify it. A dysfunctional rule is a rule that makes you constantly upset. For instance, the following rule is upsetting: "Because I am a good and faithful spouse, I deserve to be loved." Your life becomes much easier if you modify your rule requiring perfect reciprocity to something like this: "When I behave lovingly towards my spouse, he/she behaves lovingly towards me *at least a large portion of the time*. In times when he/she is not as loving towards me, I can still live normally." This way you lower your unreasonable demand, you relax, and enjoy more of your life.

Let's assume in a second example that during your studies you seek a trainee position in a company where you wish to work after graduation. You are diligent at your work and you expect that the other employees "reciprocally" like you. You also expect that the company will "reciprocally" hire you. In reality the other employees aren't necessarily accepting you with open arms. They may sense that you try to control them with your sweetness and virtuousness. When the company chooses another applicant for an open position, you are fuming because your rule of reciprocity was grossly violated.

In reality, reciprocity is a capricious state, which, at best, can be carried out only averagely because we people are so different. Reciprocity requires mediation, negotiation, compromise, and maturation as a human being. Reciprocity requires always work.

It, too, is a dysfunctional rule to think that when you work hard, you always succeed and prosper. A modified rule sounds like this: "There is no guarantee whatsoever that I succeed all the time."

You will enjoy your life a whole lot more if you dare to ease your strict rules. As you can see, easing just a few notches is sufficient.

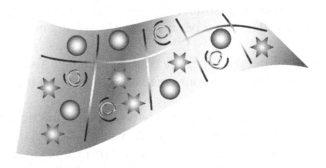

4.3 Schedule

If depression has a paralyzing effect on you, a schedule can be really useful, so you get your life back in your own control again. At a minimum, you can write on a piece of paper before going to bed or after you wake up in the morning the things you plan to do during the day. You may also choose to make a little bit more precise schedule, which has marked clock times on it. Do this even though in reality you plan to carry out only part of your plan. The plan doesn't need to be polished, and you don't need to spend more than five minutes making it.

Include both work and leisure activities in your schedule. Work is, for instance, washing a toilet bowl. Leisure activity is, for instance, playing a computer game. You may then notice that your schedule has too little or too much pleasure-generating leisure activities or that pleasure is of poor quality. As a researcher of your own life you may also make other observations.

A schedule is particularly useful in the treatment of weekend melancholy. Such weekend melancholy may bother especially single people. During the week, work keeps a single person still tied up with life, but weekend's loneliness brings along melancholy. If this is true in your case, cure your weekend melancholy by planning well in advance a detailed program for the weekend. There is no reason to think that your life has to be miserable only because you live alone.

A schedule is useful to you because then you don't ponder endlessly whether you should do something or not. Even if you get only a part of the intended work done, in all probability you'll feel satisfaction and you will proceed in overcoming your depression.

4.4 Eating an elephant in pieces

Low-spiritedness and depression are often associated with inefficiency. Sometimes the cause for stagnation is the fact that the work is immediately thought in its finished form and then the work may seem almost overwhelming. The intention is to eat an elephant, but it seems as an almost impossible mission because the animal is so huge in size. In fact, even elephants are eaten in small pieces.

Hence: chop the job into pieces and make a schedule for them.

Let's say that you are a student, and you should read your first multi-hundred-page text book written in a foreign language for an exam. The whole idea terrifies you when you leaf through the book. You find it unthinkable that you could read such a piece of brick, especially when its glossary is completely unknown to you. Remember that even this elephant is ultimately made up of tiny pieces. There are different kinds of studying techniques, and this suggestion doesn't necessarily fit your style, but one option is to work with the first chapter and test how long it takes for you to read it with concurrent browsing of the dictionary. On the basis of this one section, you can already assess the time you need to read the whole book and make a schedule based on that. Keep in mind that in the end even a textbook comprising thousand pages consists of only fifty pieces of twenty-page cakes.

A task of chopping the job means also limiting the time spent on that job. First decide how much time you spend at a time on a job and then organize something pleasant to do afterwards. It sounds simple, but it works.

Pay also attention on the way you eat an elephant. Many people stop their projects prematurely because they simultaneously bite tiny pieces from different parts of an elephant and eat until they are bloated. That is, they are trying to do too many projects or different parts of one project at the same time. For those who tend to spread themselves thin, it is better that you concentrate first on the first piece and only after eating that you move to the next.

Do you have a tendency to bite off a bigger piece than you can chew? Do you dare to put reasonable time limits for your work? When you use the elephant-eating method, you may be surprised that your efficiency is in fact increasing. At the same time your mood improves and you no longer even want to postpone your work.

4.5 Imagining and role-playing

You may apply imagining and role-playing in a number of different ways. Imagining will allow you to make big life changes, improve your mood, get relief in a difficult life situation, reduce anger, alleviate disappointment and learn discreet, self-assured, and calm behavior. You may invent even more applications yourself, you your own your life's researcher.

Suppose you want to make a big life change. You could first list the benefits for such a change. If your objective is a lifestyle renovation, you may list improved health, weight loss, and better endurance. Next you could imagine yourself in your favorite destination and the desired change has already happened. In case of a lifestyle renovation, you might see yourself swimming in the Mediterranean in Greece and wearing a swimsuit that is smaller than your current one. This kind of imagining method provides great support and encouragement in major life changes.

The next imagining method is even easier to adopt because the instruction is really short and simple: replace the movie. If your thoughts continually revolve around an unpleasant experience, in practice you are projecting a movie on a big screen of your mind, which keeps the sadness or anger alive for a long time after the actual insult — at worst even for decades. You yourself are your movie's screenwriter, director, producer, and the audience of one. You can get rid of your old horror movie by changing it to, for instance, a comedy. That, too, takes exactly the same means, mere imagination.

There is yet another option for showing bad films: turn off the projector altogether. When you find yourself watching an unpleasant film in your mind, think, or do something else. Bake a cake or scrub the bathroom or read a book or do a series of heavy push-ups or go jogging.

Imagining can be applied in a stressful life situation by labeling the situation as a temporary transition phase. It may also help to imagine that one is looking at the situation back from the future. If a boyfriend or girlfriend leaves and today it causes great sadness, in the imaginary future that ending of the relationship appears as a lot smaller blow in life.

With this kind of imagining, you can also learn, in advance, tactful, assertive, and calm behavior in situations that previously made you furious. Imagine that you ask your teenage son to take the trash out. You're asking him a number of times, yet nothing happens. At the most he whimpers something from the living room couch as he continues playing a game on his tablet. Previously you have become furious in situations like this: "Right this second! If you don't lift your behind, I will throw that gadget away!" Put your soul back into that situation, but replace your shouting with milder statements. Imagine also that you are relaxed and can't be easily disturbed. Imagine that you are tactful, assertive, and calm. For instance, you may say to your-self: "It is, of course, difficult get up in the middle of the game. There is no reason to get angry." Imagine then that you approach your son and explain the situation assertively. First you state that you already asked him many times kindly. If your son says he is tired, you can disarm him by agreeing with him. You may say that you believe he is tired, because you, too, are tired, yet you prepare the dinner for the family. After that you repeat kindly, but at the same time firmly your request that you expect him to take the trash out, because it is one of his responsibilities as a resident in the same household. Imagine in the end that your son says he finishes the game in five minutes and immediately after that he promises to take the trash out. He truly does as he promised, and you are pleased.

You may say that you don't think it is truthful to assume a positive end result, because there are no guarantees that your son will act in reality in such a mature, kind, and helpful way. You may, of course, prepare yourself also for a negative outcome. Imagine that you approach your son and he behaves in an unpleasant and arrogant way. Notice again your flared-up thoughts, replace them with more peaceful expressions, and develop a new strategy of behavior as above. Remember that change doesn't necessarily happen quickly at once, but gradually over time.

Make the most of your friends' wisdom as well. Ask them how they think and behave in certain situations that frustrate and infuriate you. You may quickly learn surprisingly lot, if only you are willing to find out.

Sometimes you also have to go against the current, that is, from imagining to reality and being practical. Especially perfectionists lower their quality of life with too high, completely imagined expectations. Then it would be practical to ask oneself, what in this situation is most important. If you are on a holiday, then the answer to that question could be relaxation, enjoyment, and recharging one's batteries. However, if you end up getting a lumpy mattress, and the holiday hotel doesn't have a new one to replace it with, you can either spoil your vacation by complaining all the time or remember that you are there to relax, enjoy, and recharge your batteries, so it would be wiser to direct one's attention from a mattress to happier matters.

Role-play or acting with friends or just by yourself can also be used for shrugging off feelings of guilt. One disadvantage of guilt is that other people can exploit it for manipulation. If you feel that you need to please other people, then family members and friends can effectively force you into doing things, the consequences of which may be harmful to yourself and the manipulator. Even though acts that have risen from guilt are very often based on idealism, the consequences may be the exact opposite.

Suppose you have a family member or a friend who takes advantage of you in many ways. He repeatedly borrows money or a car from you, forgets often to pay back his loans, and visits you for days or weeks at a time. You may think that if you asked him a favor or needed his help, he would do the same for you because loving family members and friends are supposed to help each other. If you tried to refuse, a family member or a friend might get furious and reject you. Then you really would feel guilty.

This kind of giving-in has a range of negative consequences. You participate in maintaining a dependent lifestyle, you yourself feel exploited, and the basis of the relationship is on blackmail, not love. You must constantly give in to avoid your family member or friend's rage and your own feelings of guilt.

The idea is to imagine or act out situations in which your family member or friend once again exploits you. Let's say he wants to borrow some money from you. You can practice a conversation with another friend or simply in your own mind. When you practice the situation enough, you dare to stand firm in a real situation.

It is worthwhile thinking over beforehand the principles you will plead to during the conversation. For example, you can remind your family member or friend that you have every right *not* to answer "yes" to all of his demands, and that love doesn't mean that you must always give in. In addition, try to find a seed of truth from your interlocutor's comments, because then he will be more accommodating towards continuing discussions. You'll want to adopt a determined and uncompromising position, and at the same time, be as tactful as possible. You should not fall for your family member or friend's performance in which he pretends to be helpless. It is not worthwhile responding to anger with anger, because it only strengthens a family member or friend's idea that he is a victim. Be prepared also to take a risk that your family member or friend temporarily withdraws from all dealings and prevents all contacts. Allow your interlocutor to leave the situation. Mention only that you want to discuss these issues again later. When you finally stand against your family member or friend, it often happens that he is not nearly as difficult as you had imagined in advance. He may even be relieved, and starts acting more maturely when you have set boundaries to your relationship.

By role-playing, you can practice your behavior also in a possible situation of abandonment. If, for example, your beloved announces that he is leaving you, it is not worthwhile immediately answering with accusations, because it may well turn out that your beloved is only angry and after the conversation he is appeased. Defending may, in turn, lead to a shouting match. Once again, the best solution is empathy. With empathy, you can find out the reasons why you are being abandoned. It often turns out that abandoner cares about you, but he is hurt because he feels he has been somehow left without and is afraid of losing you. Thus the abandoner is leaving you first in order to protect his low self-worth. If, instead, you hear that you're too selfish or something similar, you can try to find a seed of truth in those allegations and admit to them. You can ask for forgiveness. You can offer to repair your shortcomings and really mean it. It is, of course, possible that your beloved abandons you despite of this open discussion and your willingness to compromise. Then you can hope that your wise and mature approach will bear fruit in the future.

4.6 Mercy method

A mercy method can be reduced to three truths.
1. All people make mistakes from time to time and thus, among others, they pay too much every once in a while or make unsuccessful choices.
2. I am a human being.
3. Therefore I should from time to time get into a situation in which I pay too much or I fail in my choices.

With a mercy method, you can get rid of should statements. For instance, you may say to yourself something like this: "I shouldn't have eaten that chocolate." In reality, it was totally expected that you ate that chocolate because you have had a habit of eating chocolate already for years, if not even for decades, when you are bored or anxious or dispirited. Because you acted as expected, you only made the situation worse by condemning yourself.

If you really want to get rid of your expected habit, you succeed better with a reward than with a punishment. If you were able to resist the temptation, then treat yourself to some other, healthier delight.

You'll want to give yourself that other delight even if you succumbed to the temptation. Then it is an expression of compassion for failing. When you occasionally fail, don't spoil your pleasure by mixing it with guilt. It only provides an unpleasant off-flavor.

Another way to apply a mercy method in deleting should statements is to ask: "Why should I?" Suppose, for instance, that you hire someone to install your blinds or repair your computer. When the entrepreneur who did the job sends you a bill, you think it is higher than you had understood when you had agreed about the job. You ask about the bill, but the entrepreneur convinces you that it is totally correct and you pay it. You are, however, gnawed by a feeling that you have been taken advantage of. You berate yourself: "I should have been firmer." Ask then: "Why should I?" Perhaps you answer: "Because I always let people take advantage of me." You may notice from your answer that you don't let people *always* walk all over you, though you may work on your ability to appear more assertive. If, instead, it is true, that you always let other people take advantage of you, then you behaved exactly as expected. In order for you to get another kind of end result, you should work on a more confident way of behaving. Hence direct your energy in changing your behavior, not in berating yourself.

You are merciful towards yourself when you accept the limitations of your knowledge and inability to foretell. You might, for instance, read in the newspaper that a new ring road will be built right on the corner of the plot where you live. You understand that the value of your property will drop. You immediately think: "I shouldn't have purchased a condominium from this area. I was an idiot!" You open this trap of thought by asking a follow-up question: "Would I have purchased a condo from this area if I had known that its value will drop?" Most likely your answer is that you wouldn't have. However, you should have been able to predict the future with certainty to have behaved differently. You know very well that no one can predict the future. It is, therefore, a time for you to choose: you either hate yourself for your mistakes or accept that you are a normal, fallible member of the human race.

4.7 Desensitizing method

Desensitizing is an efficient method for especially perfectionists. Among perfectionists, there are people who think that everything has to go "exactly right." Then everyday errands and simple tasks can become nearly impossible due to too much thoroughness, stubbornness, and inflexibility. You may not see yourself as being so strict, but even you may have some compulsive tendencies. Have you, for instance, persistently tried to find a pen or a piece of jewelry even though you know it would be better just to wait for it to show up? You do it because it is so hard to stop. The minute you stop, you feel uneasy. Somehow things are just not quite right without that missing item. Alternatively, you don't feel quite right unless you check locking the door for several times.

Desensitizing helps in situations like these. First, you refuse to carry out your typical way by which you aim for perfection. Let the fear and uneasiness generated by your refusal flood all over you. Nonetheless stick stubbornly to your decision to refuse to act, even if you think you are already badly upset. After a while your compulsive feelings to act subside, until they completely vanish. This kind of struggle can take hours or as little as ten minutes. One exposure is often sufficient to permanently end a repeating habit. Sometimes you may have to repeat this method several times. Alternatively, you may think of taking a "booster shot" sometime later, that is, you repeat the method every once in a while after longer periods of time. Listen to yourself: you know yourself best or at least you are learning of becoming the best expert of yourself, and you know what works for you.

4.8 Counting method

Did you learn at some point that without constant encouragement and commanding you don't get anything done? Perhaps your parents or you yourself have labelled yourself as a dawdler. It is hard to get rid of that label if that condition has been continuing for years or even for decades. It often happens in these labelling situations that the attention is focused on things that are still undone. Then all the hundreds of things that do get done go under the radar.

In this method, the aim is to count and write down all the work and activities from one week. This way your self-confidence gets better, and you start seeing yourself as a much more capable human being. You get to peel off that old label.

A counting method is helpful also when you are dependent on other people's approval. The method is simple: you count daily positive things about yourself. Notice your positive acts and qualities even if you don't get outside approval for them. If, for instance, you smile warmly at your neighbor, it is a positive observation about you. It counts even if that neighbor keeps his poker face. Count also, as positive observations, your acts of taking care of yourself and even positive memories about yourself if they flash through your mind. In the beginning, you maybe have to force yourself to observe good things about yourself, but keep persevering. This is an incredibly simple method, but a long leap towards independence and self-acceptance.

4.9 "Oh no, I can't"

Do you see yourself as unskilled, and therefore you very often say "oh no, I can't" or "oh no, I don't know how?" Have you ever tested, if this prediction is true? Put your thoughts into a test, so you can see what the truth is.

When you appeal to the fact that you can't or you don't know how, there is often a fear in the background that otherwise you get accused of inefficiency. You try to save your skin by claiming that you're too incompetent to carry out the required task. If you repeatedly say "oh no, I can't" or "oh no, I don't know how," it becomes a habit, and after a while you've convinced yourself that you really can't. Typical "oh no, I don't know how" thoughts are: "I don't know how to make food;" "I can't drive, although I have a driver's license;" "I don't know how to apply for jobs;" "I can't concentrate;" "I don't know how to read books;" and "I don't know how to clean."

These kinds of thoughts are not only harmful to yourself but they also spoil your relationships, because others get irritated by your "oh no, I don't know how" statements. They can't understand that it really feels impossible for you to do certain things.

A very practical method is to test this prediction of yours with a real experiment. Take for instance a claim: "I don't know how to do anything in the kitchen." Surprise yourself and decide to try preparing something in the kitchen. Take for instance ratatouille, a vegetable casserole. Enter, therefore, the word "ratatouille" in a search engine, and you get immediately links to recipes. Buy the ingredients required for the recipe. Prepare a ratatouille following the recipe's instructions. If your first casserole wasn't successful, try to learn from your mistakes and prepare another one.

Several severe, chronic depressions have been cured with this simple manner.

You may hesitate testing your "oh no, I can't" or "oh no, I don't know how" statements because you don't want to take a risk of failing. When you don't take a risk, you are able to maintain your belief that in principle you are pretty capable, but this time you decide not to participate. The "I can't lose" method helps in overcoming that fear. If you truly took the risk and you fail, make a list of the negative consequences. Prove to yourself that you know how to respond constructively even if you get disappointed. Think what good could follow from a failure.

Remember also that you haven't always been a reluctant learner or reluctant in failing. When you learned to walk, you doubted, stumbled, and searched for a support many times. Still you kept on trying and finally your walking became steady.

4.10 Properly criticized

You already read from section *1.2 Self-worth and self-esteem* how you may deal with criticism by becoming unhappy, angry, or staying neutral. You remain neutral if you consider whether the criticism is justified and keep the deed and the doer apart from each other.

This method is targeted to particularly the unhappy and angry and guides how to proceed towards that neutral way. The method comprises three steps: empathy, making the critic harmless, and negotiation. Presenting an ultimatum may constitute an additional step.

Observing from other person's standpoint, that is, empathy. When someone criticizes you, he intends to either help you or to hurt you. What the critic is saying may be right or wrong or somewhere in between. In the beginning, don't focus on that at all, but ask what the critic means. Don't be judgmental or defensive, only inquisitive. Ask for as long as it takes for you to see the situation through the eyes of the critic. If your critic's comments are vague and insulting, then ask for details and accuracy. Often already this kind of settling changes the situation decisively. In the past you have perhaps attacked or become defensive, but now you are cooperating. This act also awakens mutual respect.

Making the critic harmless, that is, disarmament. If you are verbally fired upon, then you have three options. You can fire back, which usually leads to warfare and to a potential of mutual destruction. You can escape, which usually leads to humiliation. You can stay right there and make your critic harmless. It is worthwhile choosing this third option.

The critic is made harmless in such a way that you find something you can agree about with him. Hence it still doesn't matter whether your critic is right or wrong. You can agree in principle with your critic. You can find some seed of truth from your critic's speech. You can acknowledge that your critic's irritation is understandable, because it is based on his outlook. Because you find things or viewpoints you can agree upon, your angry critic usually runs out of ammunition. When he calms down, he is in a better mood to discuss rationally.

Negotiation. In the final step, you describe your views tactfully, but firmly. After that, it is time to clarify how your views differ from each other. The end result from your negotiation may be a compromise, and you have to settle for only part of what you want. If, however, you have sincerely and conscientiously empathized with your critic and made him harmless, you may get a better end result than you had even expected.

Ultimatum. Present an ultimatum only if you know that you are right and your adversary doesn't yield at all. If you threaten with a formal complaint or a lawsuit, then you have to be ready to implement your plan. Don't cultivate empty ultimatums.

As you have already learned, a depressed person often incorrectly blends a deed with a doer. It is good to keep this distortion in mind also in critique and conflict situations and only stick to the matter. It should also be borne in mind that your critic may similarly think in a distorted way. Since you, on the basis of this book, know better, your duty is to remind your critic that you both focus on matters, not people.

In many cases, it happens that your critic is right after all and you were wrong. In such a case you earn your critic's respect when you admit that he was right, you possibly thank your critic for recognizing your mistake, and you apologize for the injury or hurt feelings. If there is some financial compensation involved, you take care of it. This is old-fashioned, smart, and dignified behavior.

Finally, a reminder that if you defend yourself aggressively and vindictively, it is likely that you will not get to enjoy of constructive cooperation in the future. So even though an angry defense might feel even good for a moment, the price for that momentary euphoria can rise high. Because of your anger, you also never find out what exactly your critic tried to express. An additional price may form from the fact that you yourself suffer from guilt and punish yourself excessively because of your fit of rage. This is a wrong way to respond to criticism and predisposes to depression.

4.11 Chain of reasoning

Using a chain of reasoning is a strikingly effective method for recognizing silent assumptions.

Let's assume that your feelings were hurt because your boss gave you constructive criticism. You interpreted that guidance in such a way that the boss thinks that you are a bad employee. When you thought this way, you lapsed to mind reading. You *imagined* what your boss is thinking. You also used a mental filter, because you only remembered criticism even though your boss has praised you many times. Finally, you labelled yourself when you incorrectly drew an equal sign between a deed and a doer.

Next it's worthwhile finding through a chain of reasoning whether there are some distorted silent assumptions in the background which hinder your life. Take, as a starting point, an automatic, negative thought. That is the first loop in your chain of reasoning. Each of the even-numbered loops is always formed by the same question: "Suppose this automatic thought is true. Why does it hurt my feelings?" Below, the odd-numbered loops are answers to that one and the same even-numbered loop question. Like this:

Loop 1: My boss thinks that I'm a bad employee.
Loop 2: Suppose this automatic thought is true. Why does it hurt my feelings?
Loop 3: Because it means that I am a lousy employee. My boss is an expert, he knows.
Loop 5: Because it means that I am a total failure.
Loop 7: Then the word spreads, and everyone will find out that I am a good-for-nothing. After that no one will respect me. I'll be discharged from the working community and forced to change the field.
Loop 9: Because it means I'm worthless. I feel awful. I want to die.

When you make this kind of chain, you finally get to your silent assumptions. With this method, you peel your onion of assumptions layer-by-layer and get to its core. You can make following observations from the answers of your chain of reasoning:

1. If someone criticizes me, I believe the critic is always right.
2. I believe my worth is measured by accomplishments.
3. I believe one mistake ruins everything. If I am not successful all the time, then I am nobody.
4. I believe other people can't stand my imperfection. I have to be perfect so that people respect me. If I make a mistake, then I believe that I receive vehement disapproval and get punished.
5. I believe that disapproval means that I am bad and worthless.

If the chain of reasoning doesn't seem to be working in your case, make sure that your answers don't include feelings. Instead of feeling-type reasoning, write down the negative thoughts that cause these feelings.

Once you have found out your silent assumptions, you can begin a *conscious* work of changing them. You may benefit from reading Chapter Three yet again.

4.12 How do you tend to predict?

If you have a silent assumption that being alone is a curse, test your assumption. Then you end up to your own truth scientifically.

The method is simple:
1. Predict how much you enjoy the upcoming activity.
2. Evaluate after activity how much you really enjoyed it.
3. Make observations about yourself based on these findings.

Carry out some of the activities alone and some with someone or with a group of people. The more activities you carry out, the more reliable your study becomes.

You can learn several new things about yourself from your study. First of all, you learn about how good you are at predicting and to which direction you tend to predict. Do you perhaps have a tendency to belittle the degree of an upcoming pleasure? Or are your expectations low only in those cases when you know you will be by yourself? When you look at the realized degree of satisfaction, you learn even more about yourself. Did it happen that sometimes you were more pleased to be by yourself than with other people? You may also learn how work-related activities and leisure time activities differ from each another. This is a good piece of information because then you can better balance out your life between work and leisure.

It is, of course, possible that you do something, and it doesn't please you at the level you expected. It, too, is possible that you make a low prediction, and it is true that you do not feel any pleasure.

In such cases, you may want to check out first if the reason to your dissatisfaction is a distorted thought pattern. For instance, do you have your mental filter on? Then again sometimes a person genuinely gets disappointed without any distortions in his thinking. A fluctuation of joy and disappointment is completely expected in a normal life. This world has dark tones in a form of disappointments as well as in people's ill intentions and acrid acts. It is extremism to always try to falsely mask the truth with pastel colors and lace.

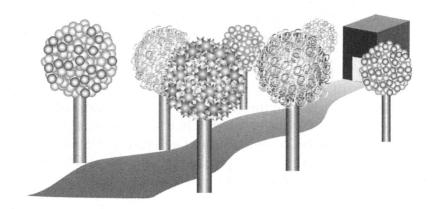

4.13 Voyage or arrival?

Old wisdom says that the journey is more important than the destination. However, a perfectionist often focuses on the end result and forgets the journey that leads to it. This partly explains the often unhappy disposition of a perfectionist.

Suppose you work in customer service. You may assume that you have to succeed in all of your customer encounters. You do have work days when you receive positive feedback from almost all of your customers. In days like that you float on top of clouds. Sometimes you, as all of us, have work days when things don't go that smoothly. Particularly grim are the days when your customers berate you. In days like that you are completely in doldrums. Thus you work in an exhausting and unpredictable roller coaster of emotions.

Why does this happen? You already know the answer that, at least partly, because you wrongfully mix a doer and a deed to each other. In addition, the second part of the problem arises from the fact that you only look at the end result. Your aim is that every customer is satisfied. If not, you have failed. You should, instead, aim for a good and consistent work effort of uniform quality in every customer encounter. This means focusing on the work itself, that is, on the voyage. If one customer gets disappointed, then you don't need to feel you failed because your performance was of equally uniform, good quality with this customer as with all the other ones. Of course you may hone your skills based on these disappointing encounters, but they don't need to affect your mood.

Being on a voyage is this life. When you feel you are travelling, you are present in this very moment, and your life doesn't slip by. It, instead, is focusing on the end result, if you live more in the past or in the future than right here and now. If you bemoan the past, you criticize the end result completed thus far. If you are already one step ahead in the future, then you try to get eagerly to the next end result. The past and the future are, however, an illusion, and reality is only this moment.

In addition, while travelling anchors you to this moment, it also brings relaxation. For instance, as a student or as a job-hunter, you know that you can only control the journey, that is, be uniformly good in your studies or job-hunt, but you can't control the end result. For a student the end result is a grade, for a job-seeker a job. When you realize this, you relax and focus your energy only on honing the quality of your travelling.

Focusing on travelling brings also flexibility. When a person working on a creative project focuses on travelling, he will be open to suggestions and enjoys learning new things. When a person working on a creative project focuses on the end result, he is tense and defensive. For the one focusing on the end result, his creative work is complete, and he has to defend it like a lioness would her cubs.

4.14 Happy-go-lucky honesty

One hatred-producing thought distortion is extremism in a form of *mind reading*. You come up with different kinds of reasons why some other person acted as he acted. Very often your conclusions don't correspond to reality at all.

The solution would be to check what the reality is, because asking may get it cleared up. Thus the instruction for this method is simple: ask directly when something is unclear to you. If your parent, spouse, teacher, employer, or an equivalent doesn't like your questions, show him this book and say that asking is included in basic instructions on being a human being.

Do you think an expert, such as a physician, is immediately bad, if he confesses not knowing and tells you he has to study more? In fact, you should feel great respect for such an expert. That's a wise and brave person who doesn't immediately pull the wool over your eyes just to save his own face. The truth is that neither of us knows it all or is able to do it all and nor should we. The expert's acknowledgement of his own not-knowing can be considered even as a mark of respect, because by doing so, he thinks of you as his equal.

If you feel nervousness and inadequacy in some circumstances, share this information with people. Show the things you feel insecure about, instead of attempting to cover up your uncertainty. Ask people for suggestions on how you could develop and improve your skills. If they reject you because of that, let them do so. If someone expresses disappointment at you or even rejects you because of your imperfection, it surely tells more about the abandoner than you.

4.15 Helping others and gratitude

Consider a possibility that you serve and help others, for instance, as a volunteer. You would then learn to give instead of taking. You would also see the spectrum of life. Serving others straightens out a sense of entitlement. Serving others is also an outward reach, and therefore, it is an opposite motion to an inward curling up of depression.

Do not take as a starting point that you serve and help others only from a sense of obligation, need for an approval, or because you're trying to be "perfect." Take empathy as your starting point. Empathy opens your heart, and your heart will expand even further in helping.

Your genuine helpfulness may at some point awaken profiteers' interest. You can get rid of them by saying something along these lines: "I will pay you a compliment. I think you'll do just fine without me. If you don't know how to do something, you can purchase the service you need."

This second method is even easier. Look around and make a list in your mind of everything you can be grateful for. What kind of abundance surrounds you? Make gratitude a daily habit. Every night before going to bed you may also think of *three things* in your day that went particularly well. This is a strikingly simple way by which people have been cured from depression.

Learn also to cultivate the expression "thank you." Saying it is old-fashioned, smart, and dignified behavior.

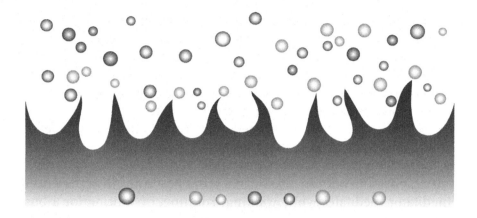

4.16 Meditation

Meditation is a wonderful gift to yourself. Meditation is silencing the production line of thoughts, but not completely stopping it, because that would be impossible and needless. In meditation, the passing thoughts are just not being clung to. Meditation does not mean dreaming. Even a mind filled with positive, dreamy thoughts is, however, a lively mind.

You already read from the beginning of this book that a brain's structures differ in meditators for their advantage from an average brain. In addition, meditation increases secretion of serotonin, which is a "happiness neurotransmitter" in the brain. Those, who have already received a depression diagnosis, know that in depression, serotonin levels are low, and this problem has been traditionally treated with medication. Meditation also reduces the body's cortisol level. Cortisol is secreted when a person is anxious. High cortisol level causes, among others, high blood pressure, obesity, non-insulin dependent diabetes, reduction in immune defenses, and fatigue. Research shows that already a twenty-minute meditation decreases cortisol level by up to 30%. Nowadays, it is no wonder anymore that a physician recommends meditation to those struggling with high blood pressure, and to those who suffer from stress, sleep problems, pain, anxiety, and depression.

In meditation, you get from a thought level to a deeper level of understanding, perception, and peace. The situation could be described by a following comparison: thinking represents the surface waves of an ocean, and meditation is the depths of a seabed, where it is completely calm. For an anxious person, those surface waves are in a continuous surge. A calm mind achieved through meditation is instead hopeful, solution-oriented, and creative. Renewed hopefulness is also a prerequisite for happiness.

You can meditate almost anywhere. Meditate preferably in a sitting position, but can also be in a lying position. An experienced meditator meditates while walking, running, or waiting for a bus. You may meditate in silence, surrounded by nature's sounds, or with music playing in the background. You are your own life's researcher, so you learn through testing what works best for you. It doesn't make any difference what others recommend, because no one knows as well as you do your own special situation, your abilities, and your needs.

Different schools teach meditation in different ways. Examples of numerous different movements in meditation are Mindfulness, Zazen, Vipassana, and Transcendental meditation. No matter what the school is, each meditation starts with relaxation. Relaxation begins by breathing deeply in and out. You can also engage in such deep breathing at other times besides before meditating. For example, an anxious person tends to be a surface breather, so he uses only the upper parts of his lungs. You can recognize that you are deep-breathing if your hand, which is resting lightly on your lower abdomen, rises and falls in a pace of your breathing. You may also relax your body by relaxing in turns different parts of your body. Start, for instance, from the toes and work your way up to the scalp. With experience, this initial phase gets reduced as relaxation becomes rapid and automatic.

When you advance from relaxation to meditation, you may keep observing your breathing, because it will take your attention away from your thoughts. When you observe your breathing, don't try to affect it anymore because affecting *is* thinking.

In Transcendental meditation, a mantra, which is given by a teacher, is repeated quietly in the mind. Mantra is a word or just a sound of a positive nature that doesn't mean or resemble anything, so that it doesn't work as a kindling for thoughts. If you want to use a mantra, it is not impossible that you choose it yourself. Calm down, stay silent for a moment, and allow a mantra to enter your mind without forcing.

If you have difficulties in silencing your mind, you can use additional resources besides monitoring breathing or repeating a mantra. You may, for instance, try if you can you feel the energy in your hands without touching anything. After a moment, most people recognize weak tingling in their hands.

When in meditation, you descend below the everyday hustle and bustle, into serenity. At the same time you also turn from a doer to an observer. A majority of people are in continuous mode of doing, being tossed around by the surface waves. Some who consider themselves as enlightened are, in turn, merely observers. They observe constantly because they fear living. This segment of doing and observing is one of the life segments presented in this book. This segment, like most of the segments, finds its balance point in the middle zone. Thus a balanced life includes both doing and observing.

Methods presented above have been developed by human beings, and you're a human being, so perhaps you will develop yet new methods or tailor the existing ones to become more suitable for you. When you do your developmental work, keep in mind the purpose of a method, which is to straighten distortions and to stay in the straightened.

5 Pieces of a puzzle and fuzzy boundaries

You were promised at the beginning of Chapter One that this book is like a sack of concrete, which allows you to cast an even foundation for yourself. You surely aren't sorry to hear that, during this foundation-casting, a load of building materials has arrived on the plot. With these building materials, you still get to build a one-story, comfortable villa. You are that villa.

The purpose of life is to become an authentic self. Everything else, which is good in this world, comes as a by-product after discovering that authentic self. One of the by-products is discovering a calling for being here on earth, a personal life purpose. Being an authentic self is like snapping as a piece of a jigsaw into a right place so that nothing abrades. When one is in the right place, the big jigsaw's image begins to take shape.

By interviewing hospice patients, *Bronnie Ware* found out that the number one regret among the patients was that they hadn't had the courage to live the life that they knew they had been destined to live. They felt there had been an internal calling, a greater purpose, a bigger reason to be here, but they had not answered to that calling. Instead, they had conformed and followed the paths already beaten by others.

Many admit that becoming an authentic self would be a desirable goal, but at the same time they say that they don't know what they really like and what makes their soul sing.

You have been closest to your authentic self when you were a child. At that point, people around hadn't yet come to affect how, in their opinion, you should be and what they expect of you. Pause to remember what you enjoyed just tremendously as a child. From those recollections, you may get some hints about who you really are.

In finding your authentic self, you may also take advantage of *Edgar Cacey*'s advice:

1. Find out the most important *basic values* for yourself. You may find them, for instance, from this group: peace, joy, honor, freedom, loyalty, creativity, integrity, positivity, efficiency, honesty, nurturing, collaboration, intellectuality, wisdom, entertainment, satisfaction, development, passion, justice, courage, education, beauty, health, awareness, adventure, conservation, protection, cleanliness, defending, truth, commerce, craftsmanship, exercise, spirituality, artistry. Various options can be found as long as you keep thinking about them.

2. Identify four to five of your most important talents, abilities, or strengths. These are the tools for implementing your vocation.

3. Develop a slogan that describes your vocation.

For example, education and freedom are important to Rita. She is a logical thinker, inquisitive, and a talented writer. Her slogan is: "I want to popularize science." Rita became a non-fiction writer, who works as a freelancer at her home.

Carl has always wanted to nurture. He is patient, attentive, and loving. Carl developed the following slogan for this vocation: "I want to help children. Particularly the sick children are close to my heart." Carl became a nurse in a children's hospital.

Finding basic values, pondering one's own talents, abilities, and strengths and developing a slogan don't have to relate to a discovery of your own career. You may also carry out your calling during your leisure time.

The next subchapter clarifies to you more, who you really are.

5.1 A human being's 16 basic desires

Social psychologists *Steven Reiss* and *Susan Havercamp* have found in their studies that a human being has 16 basic desires. They can be found from everyone and already genes determine partially which desires are strong and which are weak. In addition to genes, a person's own distorted thought patterns, silent assumptions, experiences, and environment play a strong role. It may be, for instance, that in his genes someone doesn't have a strong desire for an order, but he has whipped himself with "should" statements, and this thought pattern has affected in such a way that he has become a very neat and organized person.

It is possible to test the strengths of human desires and build a basic human desire profile on the basis of that test. Some of the basic desires are *very* important, others *less* important. Different profiles make us unique and different from each other. Hence we humans form together a vast mosaic in which each small piece is slightly different in shade, texture, size, and shape.

You get more out from the following introduction of basic desires when in each case you consider how strong it is in your own case and in cases of those close to you.

Power. Every single one of us wants at least some degree of power. Power is a desire to influence. Power motivates towards achievements, excellence, expertise, leadership, and glory.

A desire for power occurs in varying degrees. For some, it means getting a master of science degree in industrial engineering and management and then ending up a chief executive officer in a large company. A milder desire for power could be, for example, a desire to run a marathon honorably to the end, build a wooden rowboat by oneself, or even read the Bible from cover to cover.

A desire for power is a *very important* desire to you if you are more ambitious than others in your age group, you usually seek leadership roles, or you take a dominant role in social situations. A desire for power is *less important* to you if you are ambitious to a much lesser

extent than other people in your age group or if you willingly take a submissive role in social situations. Your desire is *average* if you either don't identify yourself with either group's description or if you have features from both of them. This definition for average is the same also in the upcoming sections, so it will not be repeated after this.

Independence. A desire for independence tells of a desire to rely on oneself and of a desire to be, at least from time to time, free.

A desire for independence is *very important* to you if you usually resist advice and guidance from others, or if a desire to rely on yourself is essential to your happiness. A desire for independence is *less important* to you if you are more devoted to your spouse or partner than most people in your age group or you dislike being on your own.

Curiosity. A desire for curiosity is to learn for the mere joy of learning. Thirst for knowledge and curiosity towards the unknown are represented, among others, with a desire to write, read, think, study, and explore new places. Curiosity should not be confused with intelligence. An intelligent person learns easily, but a curious person *enjoys* learning new things. Neither does curiosity mean aiming at excellent grades in one's studies. That is a desire for power.

A desire for curiosity is *very important* to you if you have a thirst for knowledge compared to others in your age group, you ask a lot of questions, or you think a lot about what is true. A desire for curiosity is *less important* to you if you dislike intellectual activities or you only rarely ask questions.

Acceptance. A desire to belong affects a person in such a way that he avoids being abandoned and being criticized. We all have a desire to be accepted as we are. Hence a gift of acceptance is the biggest and the most important gift the parents can ever give to their children. Children, who have been deprived of this gift, have low self-worth. According to Steven Reiss, a desire for acceptance is the only basic desire that is closely linked to self-worth.

A desire for acceptance is *very important* to you if you usually set easy goals for yourself, you are a quitter, you leave things undone, or you have difficulties in receiving criticism. A desire for acceptance is *less important* to you if you have high self-worth or you handle criticism noticeably better than most people, that is, you don't get unreasonably upset from it.

Order. A desire for an order is obvious when we are arranging things, making plans, writing schedules, making lists, setting rules, and when we are beautifying and cleaning up our surroundings. An order brings a sense of balance and control to people. A lack of an order can make one nervous, because disorder tells of chaos, unpredictability, and change.

A desire for an order is *very important* to you if you are considerably more organized than most people, you have lots of rules, and you follow them closely or you enjoy cleaning. A desire for order is *less important* to you if your workplace is usually messy or you don't like planning at all.

Saving. A desire to collect is saving. This desire motivates people to save money and purchase goods. Thriftiness, economy, and even tightfistedness are the keywords for this desire. Frugal people save also time because time is money. They don't want to throw anything away, because they think that there may be a need for it later. The origin for the pursuit of wealth may be in a desire to save, but wealth may be desired also in order to increase one's social status.

A desire for saving is *very important* to you, if you are a collector, a miser, or considerably stricter with spending your money than other people in your age group. A desire for saving is *less important* to you if you enjoy spending money or rarely save anything at all.

Honor. A desire for honor is a desire to be loyal to one's own parents and — by extension — to traditions, one's own ethnic group, country, religion, culture, and moral principles. A desire for honor and a strong sense of responsibility go hand in hand. People, who have a strong desire for honor, often feel guilty when they think they behaved in a dishonorable way. According to Steven Reiss, the primitive roots for a desire for honor can be apparently found from feelings of guilt.

Loyalty to one's parents is a desire for honor, loyalty to one's spouse is a desire for romance, loyalty to one's own children is a desire for family, and loyalty to one's friends is a desire for social contacts. Thus loyalty has many faces.

A desire for honor is *very important* to you if you are known as a highly principled or a very loyal person. A desire for honor is *less important* to you if you believe that everyone should ensure his own interests or you don't care much for customs, principles, and morality.

Idealism. A desire for idealism is a desire for social justice, which motivates people to participate in and contribute to the development of humankind. A person with a strong desire for idealism may, for example, be a physician in a refugee camp, but at the same time he doesn't care much for his own children. This sounds contradictory, but this is explained by the fact that this physician's desire for family is low.

A desire for idealism is *very important* to you if you make personal sacrifices for social or humanitarian causes, you repeatedly volunteer in your community's organizations and such, or you make contributions for those in need. A desire for idealism is *less important* to you if you pay little attention to what is going on in the society or you don't believe in charity.

Social contacts. A desire for social contacts is a desire to spend time with friends, acquaintances, one's contemporaries, and coworkers. A pursuit of having a good time is included in this desire. In addition to having fun, social people have a need to be with other people for the sake of their own happiness. In certain circles, joining a prestigious club or an association may rather have its origin in a desire for status or power than for social contacts. On the other hand, the origin for isolation is not necessarily in a low desire for social contacts, but for instance, in shyness.

A desire for social contacts is *very important* to you if you feel you need to spend a lot of time around other people in order for you to be happy or other people know you as a fun-loving person.

A desire for social contacts is *less important* to you if you willingly keep to yourself, you don't like parties, or you don't particularly care for other people except for your own family and a few close friends.

Family. A desire for family is a desire to raise children and love them. This desire is therefore bigger than just wanting to have children. A desire for family includes a desire to nurture and willingness to make sacrifices. However, it is not just a question of nurturing instinct, because people with a strong desire for family aren't necessarily interested in children of other people, animals, or plants.

A desire for family is *very important* to you if raising children is essential to your happiness or you spend a lot more time with your children than the other parents you know. A desire for family is *less important* to you if being a parent (or a mere thought of it) is burdensome to you, or you have abandoned a child.

Status. A desire for status is a basic desire to obtain prestige. A person who wants status wants to impress other people, he is careful of his reputation and what others think of him.

A desire for status is *very important* to you if you almost always want to buy only the best and most expensive things and you often buy things only to impress other people; or you spend great amount of time to join a prestigious club or an association and to maintain your membership in it. A desire for status is *less important* to you if you don't care much what other people think of you, you are not even closely as impressed by wealth as most people you know, or upper-class status and/or royalty doesn't make an impact on you at all.

Vengeance. There is often hatred in a desire to "get even." A desire of vengeance may appear as aggressiveness or as a competitive desire. A desire for vengeance arises when a person is offended, threatened, or it may even arise merely out of frustration when a person is prevented from getting what he wants or there are some delays.

A desire for vengeance is *very important* to you if you have trouble controlling your anger, you are aggressive, you love to compete, or you spend a lot of your time seeking revenge. A desire for vengeance is *less important* to you if you get angry slower than most people, you often ignore when you are offended, or you don't like competitive situations.

Romance. Somewhat surprisingly both a desire for sex and beauty are included in a same desire for romance. A common link for these is at least the fact that when a person wants to impress a partner candidate, beauty has its own big role in it. Appreciation of beauty includes both appreciation of physical beauty and different forms of art. When you think of an amount of time an average person takes in dissecting partner candidates, dreaming of a spouse, in courtship, having sex and, in addition, in appreciating beauty in a variety of art forms (including, among others, listening to music), a desire for romance is a significant desire.

A desire for romance is *very important* to you if you spend an unusually lot of time in a pursuit of romance compared to other people in your age group, you have a long history of sex with many partners, you have trouble controlling your sexual urges, or compared to other people, you spend much more time in appreciating beauty. A desire for romance is *less important* to you if you spend only little time pursuing or thinking about sex, or if you think that sex is disgusting.

Eating. A desire for eating is one of the basic biological needs, which is also psychologically important.

A desire for eating is *very important* to you if you spend unusually lot of time in eating or being on a diet compared to other people you know in your age group. A desire for eating is *less important* to you if you have never had any weight problems or if you only rarely eat more than you should.

Physical activity. A desire for physical activity doesn't go hand in hand with athletic talent because a human desire in this field can be great even if the know-how is mediocre. In a desire for physical activity, joy brought by physical activity is an objective in itself.

A desire for physical activity is *very important* to you if you have exercised all your life or playing some sports have an important role in your life. A desire for physical activity is *less important* to you if your life history reveals that you are physically lazy or sitting around or other inactivity has an essential role in your lifestyle.

Tranquility. A desire for tranquility is closely linked to an individual's tolerance for anxiety, fear, stress, and pain. The greater the desire for tranquility, the lower the tolerance. In the background of a degree of tolerance is partially a silent assumption how dangerous a person considers anxiety, fear, stress, and pain. A person may have, for example, a silent assumption that due to stress, he will have a heart attack, a panic attack, get mentally ill, or at least get publicly humiliated.

A desire for tranquility is *very important* to you if at least two of the following options are true: you get scared when you feel "shaky" (you tremble); it scares you when your heart beats rapidly; when you have a rapid heartbeat, you are afraid of having a heart attack; you feel embarrassed when your stomach growls loudly. Alternatively, your desire for tranquility is *very important* also if you have had recurring panic attacks or you are generally fearful and timid. A desire for tranquility is *less important* to you if you are a courageous individual, or you have far less fears than your same age peers on average.

Steven Reiss and Susan Havercamp believe that based on a young person's desire profile, one can predict, among other things, his prospective major in the university and club and association memberships. A desire profile also gives strong indication, for instance, on how religious a person is or to what extent he will participate in sports during his lifetime.

The 16 basic desires, screened from a large group of desires, are seen as final objectives, not as a means to an objective. For example, when someone likes swimming for the sake of swimming, it is all about a desire for physical activity. If someone swims a lot because he loves to compete, it is no longer a question of physical activity, but — somewhat surprisingly — a desire for vengeance.

A desire for spirituality or religion does not form its own individual desire, but it intertwines with all of the 16 basic desires. Similarly, survival is not its own basic desire, but it, too, is intertwined with others and in particular with a desire for eating.

Each desire can be looked at either as *very important, average*, or *less important*. Out of these above-mentioned sixteen desires arises then 43 million different desire combinations.

When you evaluate the importance of a certain desire in your life, it is important that you compare yourself to other people within your own age group. This is because the manifestation of desires in life changes with age. Thus, for example, a person over 50 years old may think that because he is no longer physically as active as when he was young, his desire is only average. In reality, his desire for physical activity may still be very important when he compares it to his peers in his own age group, not to the young and very active.

Still age also changes a profile. A basic desire profile is formed by the age of 14, but emphases may change to some extent with age. For young people, eating, physical activity, romance, vengeance, power, and status are usually more important desires than for the older people. A desire for family, honor, idealism, and tranquility, in turn, tend to grow in later years. Generally, these changes take place as early as at 35–40 years of age. A healthy adult's vengeance lowers already after the age of 21. Growth in a desire for tranquility is not noticeable until on average at 56 years old.

What can we conclude from all of this? First of all, a majority of people can't even imagine how diverse our human mosaic is. This simple conclusion can be drawn on the basis of people's talking and writings, among other things. It is easy to see that people consider their own desire profile as something to be aspired, and thus they are enthusiastically forcing their own solutions to others who are not, in their opinion, quite as advanced as themselves.

The fact that such diversity can't be imagined is also reflected in how much there is pure misunderstanding among people. For example, if desires for power and status are very important desires to a child's parents, it is difficult for them to comprehend why their gifted child doesn't want to study to become a physician even though the parents would pay the study costs. The parents themselves would have liked to have had such an opportunity in the past. A cautious person, in turn, doesn't understand why anyone would voluntarily climb in the Himalayas. A physically active wonders why a stationary person doesn't get uncomfortable from vegetating. A person with a strong desire for power considers easily a person with lesser desire as lazy, weak, or unsuccessful. In turn, from the standpoint of a lower desire for power, the other end of a power segment is inhabited by mere workaholics who seem to be willing to sacrifice both themselves and their families.

Between the extreme ends of each "desire segment," there is this same wonderment and condemnation. Independent people judge the dependent ones as being immature and weak. Dependent people think easily that independent people are stubborn and proud. Inquisitive people view the less curious ones as uneducated, dumb, and boring. In the eyes of the less inquisitive, the inquisitive ones are often geeks, cold, and overly analytical. Those with a strong desire for approval view the ones with a lower desire as conceited. Those who crave less approval think easily that one can find from the other end of the approval segment only crybabies, quitters, overly sensitive people and people who are immature. Each of the basic desires can be treated in a similar manner.

The more a person's own desire profile differs from a profile of another one, the lower the understanding is towards that other person. It is easier for people to understand that there are different opinions, talents, habits, and personalities rather than widely differing desires. The first big step is to understand that there are very different types of us, and our well-intentioned advice won't necessarily find much surface of contact with someone else.

Finding a common contact surface is also associated with couple formation. It has been discovered that formation of a relationship requires a similarity in desire profiles. Naturally, there are differences in desire profiles, but in a relationship those differences have to be within desires for which one is either willing to compromise or admires to other one even though he himself differs. For example, a desire for social contacts may be quite low for one party in a relationship, but he admires his partner, who has a stronger desire for social contacts. It is fine for the one with a lower desire that his partner is responsible for organizing the couple's social life.

A similarity of profiles in a relationship is generally necessary, but for three desires similarity is, surprisingly, a bad combination. These are, for both parties, a very strong desire for vengeance, a very strong desire for approval, or a very low desire for approval. Doubling these tendencies through formation of a relationship usually leads to a breakup.

One's own desire profile may explain why attempts to make life changes fail. If, for example, physical activity is not an important desire for you, then making a lifestyle renovation through physical activity may be difficult. Suppose, however, that you love music, so then you could increase your physical activity through dancing. In other words, you can harness your strong desire for romance as a draft horse for your lifestyle renovation. Reflect what kind of changes you have tried to achieve without success. Could you be more successful through some other desire, which is important to you?

Steven Reiss and Susan Havercamp's 16 basic desires left me with a number of questions and even with a difference of opinion. For example, I find it rather peculiar that sex and appreciation of arts are included within the same basic desire. Since this book has its interest mainly in distortions of thought patterns and silent assumptions and in low self-worth, we will adopt this collection as it is at this point.

5.2 Distortions of basic desires

The aim is to become an authentic self. It means, among other things, that everyone lives according to his own unique desire collection. All kinds of collection versions exist, because all sorts of versions of us people are needed to fill the wide range of life's compartments, that is, life's loci on the earth. Steven Reiss writes that the purpose of life is a sort of by-product of the fact that everyone lives according to his own basic desires. I have already proposed the same above with slightly different words: the purpose is to become an authentic self and everything else, which is good, comes as a by-product of this self-discovery.

When examining these basic desires, it seems clear that distorted thought patterns and wrong kinds of silent assumptions may affect the formation of one's basic desire collection. Then the desire collection is not authentic and it ought to be modified, so a human being has a chance to be authentic.

For every single desire, the extreme ends expose problems. These extreme ends could be described as an *extremely important* desire or a *negligible* desire. Thus even in desires, extremism takes away from balance. This phenomenon is the same as in thought patterns and silent assumptions. Based on the teachings in the previous sections and because you are your own life's researcher, you can already interpret how distorted thought patterns and silent assumptions can distort your desire profile. Thus the examples below don't cover all the options of interpretation. It is worthwhile for everyone to reflect upon what has contributed to the formation of one's own profile and whether or not it is authentic.

Disorders emphasize certain desires. Depression may enhance a desire for approval, vengeance, or tranquility. An obsessive-compulsive disorder enhances a desire for an order. An example of such compulsive activities may be constant washing of hands or straightening of carpet fringes.

Silent assumptions emphasize certain desires. A perfectionist may have an overemphasized desire for order because an order represents perfection. Behind a pronounced desire for power or status there may be, in turn, a silent assumption that performance, success, wealth, academic degrees, and titles of importance increase one's worth. An extremely strong desire for status can also be a sign of a sense of entitlement, which is based on controlling others or on taking away from others.

Low self-worth emphasizes certain desires. Low self-worth can be reflected in a strong desire for saving. A super-saver, that is, a hoarder, may sum up this desire like this: "If I let go off my stuff, I am nothing. Each piece has so many emotions and memories in it." That comment refers to feelings of worthlessness. At worst, only narrow paths form between mounds of stuff in a hoarder's residence. A strong desire for vengeance is also linked to low self-worth.

Besides low self-worth, one often finds depression and/or a personality disorder from this desire's background. Thus vengeance may be a completely unauthentic desire. It is said that a desire for vengeance can be channeled positively into a competitive desire. Is it, however, healthy even then? Is it, for instance, possible that the origin for doping, violence, and staggering compensations in competitive sports lies in a desire for vengeance? A top athlete is in sports because he either has a strong desire for physical activity or a strong desire for vengeance. Does this division also explain why some athletes show sportsmanlike behavior and some don't?

Disorders weaken certain desires. A depression may affect in such a way that a desire for independence, social contacts, eating, romance, or physical activity no longer seems very important.

Silent assumptions weaken certain desires. A person may, for example, have absorbed a silent assumption from a very religious childhood home that emphasized humility, and this is likely to quench a natural desire for power. Some people absorb from their childhood homes a silent assumption in which academic education is held in contempt. That may put a curb on an inquisitive mind. Other desires may also play a role. If, for instance, a person's own desire for honor leads to strong loyalty to his parents, and if, again, the parents hold academism in contempt, a strong desire for honor beats soundly a strong desire for curiosity. A low desire for independence may, in turn, go hand in hand with a silent assumption that makes one beg for other people's approval.

Low self-worth weakens certain desires. If a person doesn't value himself, he may forcefully shut down, for example, his innate desire for power, status, curiosity, family, social contacts, and independence.

When the purpose of life is to become an authentic self, elimination of distortions is important also from that standpoint. Thus, it is not only a question of happiness, but also of self-knowledge and the recognition of the most authentic self. Once one recognizes the most authentic self, he is able to set his goals and actions accordingly. Then one knows what he could try in his life.

Straightening distortions and modifying a desire profile to being more authentic will lead, in a natural manner, to maturation into an authentic adult, which we will look at next.

5.3 Social maturity

Social maturity, that is, maturation into an authentic adult, means that a human being acts, thinks, and carries responsibility as is expected for his age. In particular, social maturity means that we learn to see things from the other person's viewpoint. At the same time, as we are able to step within someone else's shoes, we also learn to look at ourselves from the outside. Without any judgment, we can look at the choices we have come to make and what kind of effect they have had.

With social maturation, a viewpoint expands and expands. A new wider viewpoint develops always gradually on top of the previous, slightly narrower viewpoint and from the basis of it. At the same time as the viewpoint expands, it becomes increasingly more realistic, rational, unbiased, and detached. That description may sound like a presence of a mere cold mind, but maturity includes with utmost extent also the heart. The further along a person is with his social maturity, the further along he is in the wisdom of his heart.

A child is meant to be socially immature. From that childhood immaturity a development starts, which gradually leads to adulthood's high level of maturity. Maturation is, however, halted by a chaotic and loveless childhood and the use of alcohol or drugs or both of them early on in life. When social maturity doesn't match what is expected, there will be problems to one self as well as to others, especially to those nearest and dearest.

A theory of social maturation that will be presented next has been developed by *Robert Kegan*. Kegan's theory, in turn, is based on a well-known theory by *Jean Piaget*. The original theory of social maturation has six phases, but later Kegan developed yet another four-phase theory. In this book we focus on Kegan's original theory.

The first phase of social maturation begins at birth. In the beginning, a baby believes he is without boundaries, and thus he is one with the whole world. A baby's world is just one big pudding, a sticky mess. When a baby cries for hunger and mother provides nourishment, the mother is as though one part of self to the baby, who, among other things, is responsible for food. The name for this first pudding-like phase is *Incorporative*.

Gradually a baby realizes that when he is swinging his leg, the rest of the world doesn't swing along. Surprise, surprise, to at least some extent he is a smaller entity than the surrounding pudding, who, however, has at least that swinging leg. This is how "I" or an "ego" is born. This second phase is called *Impulsive*.

Next the child understands that he is not the same thing as his desire, hunger, or fatigue, but he *has* desires. The child discovers his own desires, but is not yet able to think that others, too, could have desires. The child is also able to express his desires, and he expresses them in such a way that the tiny dictator can be welcomed into the building. This diminutive decision-maker is also already able to manipulate in order to get his way. Thus it is no wonder that this third phase is called *Imperial*.

The child tries to get his surrounding under his command, but soon learns just how far his power reaches, when parents, siblings, and family pets don't bend to every will of this diminutive decision-maker. The child wakes up to a reality that there are other people in this world, and their needs have to be taken into account. The child realizes that the needs of people, who are of particular importance to himself, should be taken into account partly for the simple reason that at the same time that enables him to get his own needs met. This is the beginning of reciprocity. This is already an expansion of a viewpoint. This is also a point when conscience is born as well as the basis for the feelings of guilt and shame. This fourth phase of development is called *Interpersonal*. At this phase the child, however, is not completely sure whose needs take precedence. Some give priority to their own needs, some to needs of the other people, and some keep changing their side back and forth like a puppet.

When a child's self-image further evolves, he realizes when he should set his own needs ahead, when let others' needs go ahead of his own. Thus a human value system is born. Values are already a more permanent basis for choices than just momentary whims, cravings, and fears. This kind of realization of beliefs, values, and principles leads to the fifth phase of maturity, which is called *Institutional*, that is, an established phase. At this phase, a child's self-image can be described with established terms. For example, a child can be described as being honest, reliable, and fair. More broadly, this established phase creates already a starting point for a society, in which moral, ethical, and legal values have an effect. A person who reaches this established phase of maturation understands the necessity for laws and ethical rules for a smooth functioning of a society. If a person doesn't reach this fifth phase of maturity, he doesn't understand the importance of laws and rules, and why he couldn't just easily choose to ignore them when so willing. This established phase is the phase of social maturation, which a typical adult reaches. A majority of adults reach this phase, although not all. For a large proportion, the maturing process also ends at this point. This is the goal for the masses in the marathon of social maturation.

It is, however, possible to mature further from this phase. Next, the sixth phase, is called *InterIndividual*. This is when a person realizes that there are more ways to be fair, honest, and courageous in this world. In the previous fifth phase, that is, in the established phase, a person had only one interpretation of what is right and what is wrong. Each person's interpretation was based on his own value system. In the InterIndividual phase, a person sees that there can be many solutions, and at the same time he understands other people's justifications and viewpoints. An individual who has reached the InterIndividual phase has the ability to think about things in a realistic, rational, unbiased, and detached way.

Take, for example, attitudes towards immigration. An individual of the fifth phase of maturity (Institutional, established) either resists or defends immigration strongly, but an individual of the sixth phase of maturity (InterIndividual) sees both viewpoints. For Institutional people, this InterIndividual people's ability to weigh and to fully understand totally opposing opinions may appear as weakness, slowness, dispassionateness, and "turncoatism."

Living as an individual who has reached InterIndividual maturity is no easy picnic. The situation would be completely different if most members of humankind had reached this phase of maturity. When an individual has to walk at the *forefront* of humanity's mainstream, it is always thankless and tiring. For this fact would testify, if only they could, Jesus, Mahatma Gandhi, Socrates, Abraham Lincoln, and Martin Luther King, Jr. who all walked at the forefront of the InterIndividual phase. As Robert Kegan himself has said: it is easy to love them after *murdering* them.

In Western societies, it is assumed that their members have achieved the fifth maturity level upon reaching adulthood, but some of the people are not yet at that stage as adults. This is not necessarily a fault of those people themselves, because bread never given can't be eaten. However, maturation is fortunate in a sense that it never has to stop unlike the growth in height. I suppose that some readers are already here and now experiencing developmental leaps.

Supposedly, more than one reader concluded after reading the description for the fifth phase that — aha! — criminals can be found from the lower phases, because they do not understand the importance of laws and rules, and therefore it is easy for them to ignore them if they so wish. This is true, and it would be easy to continue describing with examples relating to those who transgress against us all. Instead, it may come as a surprise to some that maturation up to the fifth, established maturity phase of a nicest and most good-natured person may not occur until later in the adulthood — if ever. Take, for example, a child whose parents have strict requirements and high expectations of him. Those parents believe that they are acting in their child's best interest, because they wish him a good future. In an anticipation of this good future, parents feel entitled to make choices on behalf of their child. The child tries to fulfill these wishes and he loves his parents, but at the same time he is taken aback by the negative feelings he feels toward his parents, because he himself would have had completely different kinds of interests. Out of loyalty towards his parents — being the very nice person he is — the child fulfills his parents' wills and whims. When this child reaches adulthood, he is very often at the fourth phase of maturity. He recognizes his own needs, he recognizes the needs of his parents, but he doesn't know whose needs are supposed to take precedence. As has already been mentioned, a society at large expects the fifth phase maturity from an adult, and the same expectation may in some cases also apply to a therapist if this grown-up child decides to seek outside assistance to his internal purgatory. Then therapy given from fifth phase of maturity can't find any contact surface on a patient in the fourth phase of maturity.

Note at the same time that a strong desire for honor in one's desire profile may sometimes be affected by a degree of social maturation. A desire for honor shows itself as loyalty to one's own parents. Thus it should be added that a desire profile is not authentic if it is based on premature halting of social maturation, just as a desire profile is not authentic if it is based on distorted thought patterns or false and outdated silent assumptions.

Transition to the next phase of development doesn't happen automatically, and it is not necessarily easy. It is also possible to regress in one's maturation. Maturation is often associated with pain if the maturing process happens through adversity. It is often adversity that brings a person to a standstill and makes him think and makes him want to change. When life's sandpaper rubs down the edges, it stings, and it causes pain, but at the same time those edges become rounded and the surfaces more satiny. At best, the sanding does the same to a human as it does to a wooden piece of furniture: it becomes more refined.

Why should one suffer from maturation pains if it is possible to just stay stagnant? Although climbing the maturation ladder can sometimes be painful, otherwise life on every single step upwards becomes clearer and happier. For example, at higher maturity levels, there isn't a need to fiercely defend one's own opinions, because the expanded viewpoint allows also other people's opinions. That alone brings peace and balance into life. Besides, staying stagnant doesn't save from pain. On the contrary, staying stagnant is both painful and chaotic.

Adversities never go away, but with a higher degree of maturity, some of the setbacks seem pretty insignificant. On higher levels of maturity, one can also see the opportunities presented by adversity more clearly when fruitless whining, slander, brawling, destruction, and vengeance turn into productive problem solving. Therefore, it is worthwhile maturing.

5.4 Fallacy of control

Have you, by any chance, noticed one really interesting commonality as you have been reading this? In the beginning of social maturation, there is this pudding-like fallacy of control, and in distorted thought patterns there is this pudding-like fallacy of control.

For a baby, the whole world is one big pudding (a sticky mess). It takes time for a baby to see that when his own hand is moving, the other things in his visual field are not moving at the same time and at the same pace. Thus the hand is separate from the rest of the world! The hand is also something that "I" manages, because the hand swings when the baby wants it to. This is how the baby slowly differentiates itself from the pudding into a separate "grain of sand" with fixed boundaries. Hopefully at some point of his life, he sees himself as part of a huge sandy desert, not the only grain of sand in the universe.

Let's look back at that fallacy of control included in thought distortions. In it, in a similar manner, the space between people is mere pudding. In a fallacy of control, human's ego boundaries swallow up other people inside of them, and a person imagines he is allowed to and able to control others, though he shouldn't control anyone but himself. Alternatively, when another person invades within one's own boundaries, a person believes that that other person certainly has the full right and power to control him. If a person holds other people under his control or as rulers of himself, he has a distorted perception that others are somehow part of him. Even though it may not have been mentioned for every such thought fallacy, the majority of fallacies in the fallacy of control family were *narcissistic* thought distortions.

Thus it seems evident that some people don't properly bud from the pudding and turn into a grain of sand. One's own boundaries stay gauzy, foggy, pudding-like. Something has happened at a very early stage that has interrupted social maturation. There either wasn't love or for whatever reason it didn't convey to a child. That, too, is possible that the genetic composition or developmental disorder of a child caused an inability to accept love. Perhaps a parent himself never received love, so he didn't have anything to give. Alternatively, there was love, but the continuing chaos and unpredictability displaced love. Did parents' fears, a child's own fears, or both their fears go perhaps before love? Reasons could only be guessed, and no one knows the definite answer.

This observation of a fallacy of control doesn't seem to be a coincidence. According to Robert Kegan, social immaturity has its share in a number of mental disorders. In fact, social immaturity *is* a basis for a mental disorder. This is fully in line also with the notion by M. Scott Peck that growth in mental health and growth in spirituality is one and the same thing. Unless social maturity and spirituality is one and the same thing, at least they have commonalities. For instance, both a socially mature person and a spiritual person have an advanced capacity for empathy.

Robert Kegan states that social immaturity is associated with "cluster B" personality disorders, which show dramatic and unpredictable behavior. This B-cluster consists of four separate members: antisocial, borderline ("black-and-white and unstable"), histrionic ("attention-seeking"), and narcissistic ("grandiose") personality disorder. According to Robert Kegan, social immaturity is apparently also associated with "cluster C" personality disorders, which show anxiety and fearfulness. This C-group has three separate members: an avoidant, dependent or an obsessive-compulsive personality disorder. In addition to social immaturity, people with personality disorders carry the burden of a heavily distorted way of thinking.

Researchers claim that people with a personality disorder have often, but by no means always, low self-worth. If self-worth is low, it may even be very low. I tend to think that people with a personality disorder have *always* low or even very low self-worth, but some of them may have high self-esteem, which is only an icing on top of the core, self-worth. When a person has high self-esteem, he knows he is good, competent, and compares well to others in numerous things, and therefore he feels quite good about himself. That esteem-icing is so pretty and intact that he never even realizes his low self-worth until a major setback scratches that pretty surface and the core gets exposed. Low self-esteem has, though, already revealed its own existence many times before in countless little choices, habits, and thoughts.

Personality disorders are an extreme phenomenon. Hence personality disorders are situated on an extreme end of a life segment. This time it is a question of a *segment of responsibility*, which will be presented next. Personality disorders are paired with anxiety disorders on the other extreme end of the segment. Once again, health and balance would be found by a subtle movement towards the center.

5.5 Segment of responsibility

M. Scott Peck has introduced a segment of responsibility in his renowned classic *The Road Less Travelled*. M. Scott Peck believes that at one extreme end of the responsibility segment are those with an anxiety disorder and on the other extreme end are those with a personality disorder. Those with an anxiety disorder are too responsible and, in turn, those with a personality disorder avoid responsibility. When life of a person suffering from an anxiety disorder becomes complicated, he automatically thinks he himself is guilty for it. When life of a person suffering from a personality disorder becomes complicated, it is always someone else's fault or a system's fault and he himself is a victim.

As the name indicates, those with an anxiety disorder suffer from anxiety, tension, and fear. Anxiety manifests itself in the body, for example, as sweating, heart palpitations, shortness of breath, insomnia, dizziness, nausea, and abdominal pain.

Those with a personality disorder have, in turn, stubborn, awkward, and rigid ways of behavior, which cause suffering both to themselves and their environment.

In the context of this responsibility segment, it is worthwhile focusing on cluster B personality disorders, which reflect dramatic, emotional, and erratic behavior because identification of their kind is part of the basic instructions on being a human. If one learns to recognize them, one may avoid a lot of hardship and sorrow.

A commonality for cluster B personality disorders is self-centeredness and scarcity or total lack of empathy. Lack of empathy refers to an inability to put oneself in another person's shoes. When a lack of empathy is described through a crass example, it means this: if a normal person sees another person's leg being pressed under a massive weight in an accident, he would be horrified knowing the kind of pain the victim is suffering and would attempt to help. A person who is completely incapable of empathy could calmly follow the destruction of the other person's leg. He doesn't understand that the victim is in pain because he himself is not hurting anywhere.

If he helped, he would help only because he thinks it is expected of him in the light of the general rules of morality.

A person with an *antisocial personality disorder* acts according to his own interests, can be treacherous, irresponsible, violent, and reckless. Some antisocial people are psychopaths and sociopaths. Psychopathy is considered congenital, sociopathy is thought of being caused by the environment. In addition, sociopaths' emotional life is considered more unstable, and their behavior more erratic and impatient than that of psychopaths. In turn, a psychopath is capable of behaving more methodically. Both psychopaths and sociopaths are incapable of repentance, but perhaps they are, however, less blinded by delusions of grandeur than narcissists. *Paul Babiak* and *Robert Hare* have also introduced a concept of corporate psychopaths. These are successful climbers who operate in many disastrous ways in corporations, organizations, and in politics.

A person with a *borderline personality disorder* has black-and-white and unstable behavior, which means, among other things, constant rowing, towing and shilly-shally going — sometimes loving, sometimes hating, sometimes begging to return, and sometimes yelling to finally clear off. Therefore, break-ups are typical, but at some point a borderline person may return to a relationship as if nothing had happened, without any apologies.

A person with a *histrionic personality disorder* seeks attention, that is, he behaves as if he is constantly living on a theater stage or in an action movie. He wants all of the attention to himself, his expression of emotions may be exaggerated, seductiveness inappropriate, his interests are in his own attractiveness and his emotions are superficial and variable.

A person with a *narcissistic personality disorder* sees himself as being better than other people and therefore he thinks he is entitled to a special treatment and admiration from others. Other people are footboards to a narcissist as he journeys towards his own personal gain. At the same time, he abandons people who are useless to him and gathers a loyal admirers' court around him. In order for a narcissist to maintain an image of his own superiority and entitlement, he is cunning, lying, suffers from envy and is ready to retaliate. He may also maintain his illusion of superiority with an arrogant attitude. A narcissist's style collection may also include candied words or enticement. A narcissist also masters a manipulative way to cry to get his way. When a narcissist is caught in an act of crime or something similar, he may cry out of self-pity, not because of the pain experienced by potential victims. On the other hand, a narcissist is, if he so chooses, able to be completely matter-of-fact, charming, pleasant, interested in the person he is talking to, happy, funny and entertaining. Therefore, it is difficult to identify him.

These four cluster B personality disorders would not be in a same group, unless they had some commonalities. Hence these descriptions, which from the outset are incomplete, may fit partially also to another personality disorder in this same group.

Unpredictability associated with these personality disorders is a mechanism by which close people can be conditioned for certain kinds of behavior. When one never knows what direction the wind is blowing from and how fast the wind changes or intensifies, the close ones may strive for marked calmness and often learn to "walk on eggshells". So the close ones are wary of their words and actions, they arbitrate, reward, give in, quiet down and humble themselves. The close ones are afraid to be who they really are. If they happen to dare, the end results are conflicts, retaliations and possibly mutual abandonment. As part of the unpredictability of a personality disorder is the fact that often the wind blows from the south, warmly. Then a personality-disorder-sufferer praises and rewards his close ones and seems affectionate towards them. The close ones live in a constant hope that it would wind once again from the south. Anticipation of the south winds helps them also to cope.

Personality disorders of cluster B resemble closely the description of the "pudding-like" early phases of social maturation and also the third Imperial phase. In that third phase, a family's little dictator already recognizes his own desires, but not the desires of others.

Early phases of social maturation should only be temporary phases in human development on a way to adulthood. However, for some people, social maturation clings to these early phases for a long time or for an entire lifetime. At the same time, intellectual development and acquisition of social *skills* can be perfectly normal. People with a cluster B personality disorder might be similarly able to mature and change like anybody else, but they usually either don't acknowledge the problem or they don't want to change They do not feel the need for a change because they feel that other people are to be blamed for their misfortunes and feeling bad. Some of the people with a personality disorder may acknowledge their disorder, but even consider it as a strength in coping with life. However, the fact remains: they are often subject to adversity just because of this immaturity. In addition, even the most intelligent of them can only dream of wisdom. After all, intelligence and wisdom are not the same thing. If they recognize and acknowledge having this disorder, it is possible for them to continue on the path of maturation. It is an open path for everybody. The route for maturation doesn't even have a "best before date," but one is allowed to and can mature until the end of one's life.

A representative of the other end of the responsibility segment, a person suffering from an anxiety disorder, carries too much responsibility and sees the fault always in himself, so he, in turn, is easy to treat in therapy.

A person can, at the same time, suffer from an anxiety disorder and a personality disorder. Then in some areas of his life he carries responsibility not belonging to him, which manifests itself, among others, as feelings of guilt. In some other areas of his life he avoids responsibility, which clearly belongs to him.

A large proportion of people suffer from some anxiety disorder or some personality disorder or both in different areas of their lives. M. Scott Peck has pointed out that in a way all children suffer initially from a personality disorder. The fact is that children instinctively deny their responsibility and involvement when they get into trouble. When the mother asks siblings about who started the dispute, both are usually eager to accuse the other one. You could already conclude yourself this children's normal personality disorder based on Robert Kegan's theory on social maturation.

That previous finding by M. Scott Peck on children is an excellent introduction for extending the traditional description of narcissism. Many people assume that they could quite easily recognize a narcissist in real life. People with such an assumption have a stereotypical perception that a narcissist is like an old movie gangster or a temptress. One could immediately tell from those that the character's intentions are not going to be simply benevolent.

I think some narcissistic adults could be called *puerile narcissists* with a reason. Puerile comes from a Latin word, which means childishness. Such a puerile narcissist is as though a more benign version of a wily narcissist, which itself is far too stereotypical description. An adult puerile narcissist may be in a childlike manner endearing, open, enthusiastic, funny, entertaining, often flattering and in some cases even of high moral values and ostensibly helpful whose narcissistic traits don't come clearly out until mainly in conflict or competitive situations. Because any form of a narcissist doesn't usually have feelings of shame, a puerile narcissist may then reveal his thoughts in a strikingly direct way, and seeking for his own self-interest. For example, if a female, middle-aged puerile narcissist takes a fancy to a man and it turns out that the man is, in fact, more interested in her friend, a puerile narcissist is not at all embarrassed to pour out her disappointment by criticizing her friend with harsh words of all her qualities and even old life choices. Then she reveals how she has already previously labelled her friend in her mind as inferior to herself, and thus she can't grasp why she herself didn't get chosen although in her own opinion she is the better, more beautiful, more successful, wealthier, and a more intelligent choice. With her austere estimate, she also declares that others were at fault, not her, and she was wronged in that situation. A puerile narcissist is difficult to identify, because even in a close relationship identification may take years and requires a clear conflict or competitive situation in which a puerile narcissist is perhaps for the first time being defeated. If a friend is so wide awake that she eventually identifies a puerile narcissist, she usually finds in retrospect that several little strange events finally get their explanation. Bewilderment may have already earlier arisen from numerous deviations from the truth, constant comparing, instigation of uncertainty in another and almost imperceptible exploitation. These are mechanisms by which a puerile narcissist shows that she is always a winner in her close relationships. If she wasn't a winner, she would be a failure and worthless.

In a sense, all children also suffer partly from an anxiety disorder, that is, they take responsibility that doesn't belong to them. For example, if a child doesn't receive love from his parents, he assumes that it is his fault and he doesn't deserve love, even though it may be a question of parents' inability to love. Same applies to a young person who fails in his first dating relationships. This young person feels he is a failure and he is pretty useless. Only maturation into authentic adulthood helps to mitigate such a dramatic outlook. In an authentic adulthood, self-worth is high, capacity for empathy is advanced, and distortions have been straightened.

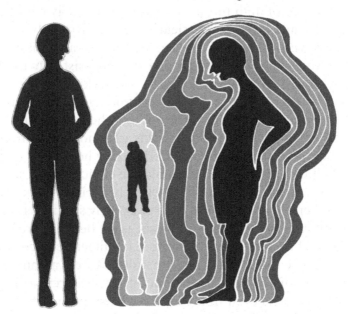

Imagine for a moment of a person whose clear, tight boundaries of control run "skintight" along his contours. Such a person understands that he controls his internal space and takes responsibility for it. Imagine then gauzy human boundaries. They are exactly that pudding or fog. These kinds of boundaries spread easily outwards, but they can also shrink inwards. It is very possible that a person with "pudding-like" boundaries, whose boundaries spread outwards, meets a person with "pudding-like" boundaries, whose boundaries have shrunk inwards. A spreader conquers that shrunken space. These kinds of two people can create a union in which one completely controls the other. Of course, other combinations of "pudding-like" people are also possible. Two spreading narcissists may be drawn together, for example, by their distorted desire profiles. As you remember, a degree of similarity between desire profiles generally gives a good expectation value for the permanence of a partnership. For example, both narcissists' strong desire for power and status may be the common factors — and the basis for building a family.

Parents with a slight anxiety disorder are better parents than parents with a personality disorder. Parents with a personality disorder push even in their childrearing their own responsibility to others and are the first to blame each other, school, society, their own relatives, neighbors, justice system, media, and the other children for their own children's mistakes. Parents with a personality disorder push responsibility also to their own children. They do that by saying that they would have studied more and thereby they would have been more successful in life if they had not been mistaken to have children. They can also blame their children for their unhappy marriage. There are tens of different ways to impose responsibility and judgment on the child. If parents with a personality disorder have several children, they often separate them in such a way that they are either "chosen ones" or "scapegoats". The chosen ones receive praise and support, but at the same time they have the greatest pressures to succeed. Often the areas of success are chosen by the parents themselves, so they can live vicariously through their chosen children. The children who have been chosen to be the scapegoats, are, in turn, blamed, belittled, and discriminated. Children may end up being scapegoats for the simple reason that expectations were set for them to be perfect wonder children, but the children behave normally in a manner appropriate for their age. The chosen children may feel resentment towards the scapegoat children because they got away with a lot less pressure. The scapegoat children may feel bitterness towards the chosen children because they attracted all the attention and praise from the parents — and they themselves received nothing. The chosen children learn that they are worthy only through their accomplishments. The scapegoat children learn almost from the beginning that they are worthless. Hence neither ones get genuine self-worth. Because of their own behavior, parents with a personality disorder often raise children with either a personality disorder or an anxiety disorder. If other caring and mature adults have been able to participate in the childrearing process in one way or another, the fate can be avoided. One can also change his fate later — for instance you are doing it right now by reading this book.

A person with a personality disorder, who behaves charmingly, may be very difficult to identify, so one should not blame himself if such a person ends up becoming one's spouse. Sometimes, however, the warning signs are foreseeable. Then one should not be wide-eyed and believe in "healing" the other one with love. No one can be cured without a person's own will and desire. No one is supposed to change anyone but himself. One can provide tools for a change, but there shouldn't be an assumption that the other one accepts them. This kind of "healing with love" is just as much a fallacy of control as any other fallacy of control.

When a person limits his control to himself, it doesn't mean that he is indifferent towards others. On the contrary, solid and right-sized boundaries of control are a sign of a high degree of maturity and a mature human being feels that we are one. A mature human being, if anyone, cares about how we cope as a whole.

5.6 Empathy, control, and responsibility

In the beginning of social maturation, a human being is unable to slip into another person's shoes and look at things from his point of view. Upon maturation, the point of view expands and expands. Thus the basic formula for social maturation is: the broader the perspective, the higher the degree of social maturation. This basic formula can be also expressed this way: the broader the perspective, the more authentic the adult.

You already know that stepping into another person's shoes and a change in perspective represent empathy, which was discussed in section *1.3 Empathy*. Hence scarcity or a total lack of empathy represents social immaturity.

How, then, can you proceed in social maturation? By developing your capacity for empathy. Doesn't it sound a bit contradictory that from a sticky pudding buds a grain of sand in such a manner that one slips into another person's shoes? You would imagine that the totally opposite happens. You would imagine that if you examined the world from other people's perspectives and began to understand how they think and feel, then isn't that exactly how a grain of sand melts into a complete pudding. This is by no means the first and the last contradiction in life.

You do remember from the beginning of this book that empathy is a skill that everyone is able to learn. It can be practiced. You are not held back from your capacity for empathy by anything else but lack of practice. Practice means repetition and perseverance, not a quick, one-time experiment. Thus, you may also be held back from your capacity for empathy by giving in too early. Do not give in.

Practice by thinking of somebody close to you and think of some decision he arrived at, but which you disagreed with at that time.

Think of this situation now again in such a way that you imagine standing in his boots. What were the conditions that surrounded that situation? You still don't have to accept his decision, but only to understand his thinking and the circumstances of that time and preceding it, that led to the decision.

Next, think how your own behavior has influenced another person in some meaningful life situation. This other person may be your spouse, parent, sibling, child, friend, or coworker. This may prove to be a more burdensome task if you notice that you had a negative and at the same time perhaps even a significant effect on this other person. Your actions may provoke remorse, but at the same time it is a sign of maturation. You are experiencing maturation pains. At this point you dare to experience this pain because you have already advanced to a stage in your distortion-straightening where you can bear that pain. It no longer throws you to years of guilt and self-denigration. You know that it also is worthwhile remedying the situation if it is remediable. If not, this experience remains to serve you in your own maturation.

Perhaps you are exactly now in a situation where your actions and your decisions affect significantly another person's life. Are your actions and your decisions perhaps negative? In your opinion are they just a little mischief? Step into the shoes of the subject. Do your actions represent only a small annoyance from his point of view or do they have a crucial effect on the rest of his life? I am especially speaking to parents whose children have ended up becoming pawns in the middle of a divorce. I am also speaking to bullies at homes, schools, workplaces, and online. I am also speaking to people who are in a position of power in their work.

Don't limit your empathy practice to only people. What would it be like to be one of three schnauzers in a two-room apartment where human tenants are at work all day long?

When social immaturity is seen as narrowness of perspective, empathy, indeed, provides a path for maturation. With the help of empathy, it is possible to bud from a pudding into a clearly defined grain of sand. When social immaturity is seen as a fallacy of control, clearing one's boundaries provides a path for maturation.

One simply has to internalize the facts: my boundaries end at me, I control only myself, I don't control others, and others don't control me. When social immaturity is seen as a slippage into an extreme end of the responsibility segment, moving more towards the middle offers a path for maturation. In practice, this means that a person with a personality disorder must take more responsibility and a person with an anxiety disorder less responsibility.

When a person with a personality disorder lays blame and responsibilities on his close ones, his starting point, neighbors, colleagues, civil servants, organizations, media, the state, the whole world or fate, he, at the same time, unknowingly gives up his power and freedom. This sounds totally opposite to how a narcissist, for example, communicates with his appearance. A narcissist does regard himself as a superior relative to other people. Perhaps a narcissist has to be arrogant — or at least quietly and secretly arrogant — on a conscious level, because at an unconscious level he has long since given up his power and freedom.

Full power and freedom, however, belong to a person who dares to make conscious choices and carry an appropriate amount of responsibility. A person can maintain full power and freedom by making these conscious choices constantly.

In particular personality disorders have become, to some extent, even admirable in some people's eyes. The reason is that in movies and reality television distortions and social immaturity create drama and dangerous situations. They are entertainment. Although you should not live under an erroneous premise that social maturity brings dullness and boredom. Even Jesus knew how to overthrow the tables of the moneychangers and drive the merchants out of the temple. It must have been dramatic. Still screenwriters in the entertainment industry are right: distortions and social immaturity generate drama with continuous, intense pace and it is often totally absurd, and therefore it is entertaining to some audiences.

5.7 A small and big paint brush

Human maturation has an interesting arc: first everything is one big pudding, then a person buds from the pudding into a separate grain of sand and finally he returns back into a sort of a pudding. How so? Along the long maturation process, that grain of sand realizes that he is only a part of a sandy desert. How does a sandy desert look like from a distance? It sort of looks like a pudding, but these two puddings differ from one another. When the first one is watery and boundless, the second one is rather like a gritty semolina pudding.

When the perspective of a grain of sand has expanded more and more, he finally realizes that he is just a chip of a large same. He is then one with everything. This stage can be called a very high degree of social maturation or phase, where a grain of sand, piece by piece, gives up his "self" or ego. A person approaches "egolessness." For example, *Eckhart Tolle* teaches social maturation in terms of first having an ego and then giving up an ego.

Many would like to be on a high level of social maturity. They think that it means that one approves lovingly everything and then they attempt to act accordingly. This is a misunderstanding and behind it is partly the nature of the word "understand." It is one thing to understand how another one thinks, but it is another thing to accept how another one thinks. When one understands the other person's viewpoint, it only means that he can see and think and perhaps even feel as the other one does. It doesn't require accepting harmful acts of that another one and leave them unpunished, because one "understands" the other one. This is just as extreme as the other end: favoring excessively cruel punishments. The truth in this case, as usual, is found somewhere from the golden middle.

Robert Kegan's theory's fifth phase of social maturation was the level, which is reached by a number of adults living a balanced and happy life. However, at that stage, the person is still a grain of sand, which doesn't see the immense sandy desert, even though he can already see and experience, if necessary, through the eyes of others. When a person is a differentiated, small grain of sand in the fifth phase of maturation, he paints with a small brush. When painting with a small brush, one sticks to rules, formulas, settlements, limitations, clauses, sections, articles, quarterlies, and memos. A small brush paints lots of small details and then simple things grow easily into difficult, complex, and unreasonably big and important matters. Besides humans, also companies, organizations, and even entire countries may end up painting mostly with a small brush.

The fifth phase includes blind compliance with laws and regulations. On the sixth stage, one is already more awake. How do a fifth maturity level pedestrian and a sixth maturity level pedestrian behave at traffic lights? In the initial situation, the light is red for both of them. However, the street is empty, that is, there are no cars in either direction. A person of the fifth maturity phase obeys the law and waits obediently for the lights to change on a desolate street. A person of the sixth maturity phase asks himself why the traffic lights exist in general from a pedestrian's point of view. He answers to himself that in order to protect the pedestrians and to enable them to cross the street. Since there are no cars, he needs neither protection nor enabling. Thus he dares to cross the street, even if the light has not yet changed to green. This example is not an invitation to civil disobedience, but rather an encouragement for using one's brain.

However, an even greater wisdom may be to follow the rules, even though one realizes them being purposeless in certain situations. For example, a pedestrian of the sixth maturity phase obediently waits for the lights to change on a desolate street if he has an unfamiliar child on his side who is not yet at a similar maturity level. Otherwise the child might later get in danger because he only learned a pattern of behavior, not the reasoning behind it.

Although a person of the sixth maturity phase would sometimes think that certain rules are purposeless, he can comply with them also for the reason that it is often wise to choose one's battles. Sometimes giving-in and compliance show more wisdom than adherence to one's own principles.

How do a person on a low maturity phase and a person on an advanced maturity phase react when a loved one is dying of a very painful and incurable disease? A person on a low maturity phase prays or hopes that the loved one doesn't die. The subject of the prayers or hopes is first and foremost his own desire to keep the loved one and a fear of being left alone. A person on an advanced maturity phase may pray or hope silently that his loved one would already get out from this earthly plane. A person on an advanced maturity phase is able to stand in the loved one's shoes, and he knows how much the loved one is suffering. A person on an advanced maturity phase loves his loved one so much that he hopes him peace and the ending of pain.

If a larger portion of humanity would rise to the highest phase of social maturity, life would be painted with a bigger brush. Simple things would remain simple, rule-blindness would change to vision, and humanity would get into solving its real problems.

The following story is based on a real person, *Jon Jandai* from Thailand. This story is not suggesting that all of us should live like Jon does. This story is here more as a food for thought, own thought. It is also an example what it looks like to paint with a bigger paint brush.

When Jon Jandai was a child, everything was fun and easy. Then he was told he is poor and he should do something about it. So Jon moved from his poor Thai village to Bangkok. He studied a lot and worked hard. Even though he worked hard — at least eight hours a day — he didn't get enough to eat and had to share a small room with a lot of people. Jon started questioning, why is it that when he worked hard, life became hard. Shouldn't his life have become easier?

In order to improve his life Jon was taking courses in architecture and engineering at the university. He learned how to cover good land with more and more concrete. Then he took courses in agriculture and learned how to poison the soil and water. Jon made a conclusion that we make everything very complicated and hard. We make life very hard. Jon felt really disappointed.

Jon reminisced his childhood when life had been fun and easy. No one in his village had ever worked for more than two months a year. Planting rice took one month, harvesting it another. For the rest of the time — ten months a year — they had been enjoying the numerous festivals and daily naps. When people had all this free time, they had time to be with themselves and understand themselves. When they understood themselves, they saw what they really wanted in life. Usually they wanted only happiness, love, and beauty. Some expressed this beauty by carving fine, elaborate knife handles, others weaved beautiful baskets. Now everyone just used plastic.

Jon decided he couldn't live this way. He quit his studies, moved back to his childhood village and started living like the villagers, working two months a year. From this work, he got four tons of rice a year. His whole family, six people, ate less than half a ton per year so there was excess rice to be sold. Jon dug two fish ponds, so there was enough fish to eat for a whole year around. Jon also started a small garden, less than half an acre, and spent fifteen minutes a day taking care of it. That garden produced more than his family could eat, so Jon started selling some produce as well. Jon thought this was easy. He had worked very hard in Bangkok for seven years, but didn't get enough to eat. Now he barely worked at all and had food in excess.

Jon had noticed that people who had had the best grades at school — unlike him — had to work 30 years to get a house. So how could he, a college drop-out, ever get a house? Then Jon tried earthen building and it, too, was easy. He only spent two hours a day doing construction work and already in three months he had a house to himself. It was so easy. Jon has since kept building at least one house a year.

Previously Jon had thought he had to have fancy clothes to become a better, more handsome man. He had used a whole month's salary to buy a pair of jeans. Those jeans had been expensive, but Jon still saw the same man in the mirror. Jeans didn't change his life. Jon figured it is not smart to follow fashion. If you start following, you are always a follower. You never catch it. Since then, Jon has not bought clothes. He now uses clothes other people give him. In fact, he has been given so many clothes that he has to keep passing them on to other people. It is so easy.

In the beginning, Jon had worried about getting sick because he had no money. Then he contemplated that sickness is a normal thing. The role of sickness is to remind us that we are doing something wrong and it's time change old habits. So Jon learned to heal himself. He thought, again, that life is very easy.

Jon felt free. Jon didn't worry much about anything. He had less fear. He could do what he liked. Before he had had a lot of fear and couldn't do much anything. Now he was thinking that he is a unique human being, and there is no one like him on this earth. There was no need to make himself like anyone else.

Because in Bangkok Jon had been in a very dark place, he figured there are other people who are now in a similar situation. Thus Jon started a center for self-reliance and organic farming. The main aim there was to save genetically unmodified seeds. There is no food, no life, unless there are seeds. No seeds, no freedom. No seeds, no happiness, because then you depend on someone else. Jon also established a learning center for all to learn how to make life easy, because we have only been taught how to make life complicated and hard.

Life is easy, but we don't know how to make it easy anymore. We have also been taught to disconnect from everything else and to be omnipotent, so we can rely only on money. To be happy, we have to connect to ourselves, to connect mind and body to one another again. We also have to connect to other people again. Jon thinks that the four basic needs — food, housing, clothes, and medicine — must be cheap and easy for everybody. That is civilization. It is uncivilized to make people work really hard to get them. If you look around, everything is so hard to get. There are currently more universities and cleverer people on the earth than ever, yet life is harder and harder. Jon doesn't think it is normal. We should go back to normal. A bird makes a nest in a day or two, a rat digs a hole in one night, but a clever, educated human being spends 30 years to pay off his house. Then there are a lot of people who believe they can never get a house.

For Jon it is enough to have a normal life, even though people seem to think Jon's way is an abnormal way. Jon doesn't care what they think. For Jon life is easy and his mind is light. Jon believes we all have a choice: to have it easy or to have it hard.

5.8 Important pieces of a jigsaw puzzle

Becoming an authentic self has, in addition to personal happiness, importance for the whole of humanity — or in fact for life of all organisms. When the pieces fall into their proper places in a huge jigsaw puzzle, the picture begins to take shape. When one latches to the right place, abrasion ends. When abrasion ends, continuous complaining and moaning ends.

In a jigsaw formed by more than seven billion people, it is difficult to see the importance of one's own piece the same way as in a closed, small community. Still, a closed small community is, after all, only a miniature model of something really big.

Let an Antarctic research station be our model for a closed, small community. It is literally a closed community for half a year, every year. During the Southern hemisphere winter, the conditions are such that there is no arriving or leaving the continent. Even dropping fresh supplies from over-flying planes is considered dangerous. People on the continent have to prepare carefully for that half-year of continuous darkness, shredding breezes, and unimaginably low temperatures. Many people don't come to think of it, but in addition to the aforementioned severity, even the oxygen levels are low because the Antarctic research stations are located high above the sea level.

Especially during the isolation period, every human being on the research station plays an important role. If one link fails, the entire community may be at risk. Some members of the community have the responsibility to calculate the nutritional needs for the whole community and reserve meals for half a year. Some members are primarily responsible for electricity and heat, but in case of emergency, each member has to be able to use the generators. Maintenance of cleanliness, hygiene, and waste treatment based on recycling has its own challenges. A number of mechanical, life-enabling devices require a maintenance worker and a repairman. If there are problems and they can't be solved, the community is in a danger to perish.

In 1999 physician *Jerri Nielsen* was in charge for healthcare at an American research station. The station's winter occupation at that time was 41 members. In the middle of the half-year darkness and isolation, Nielsen felt a lump in her breast. Because she was the only physician at the station, she trained other members to assist her in taking a biopsy from her. A pathologist in the United States made a diagnosis based on the microscopic images of that excision. As Nielsen had feared the diagnosis was breast cancer. Nielsen received cancer drugs to the station via an exceptional and dangerous over-flight delivery. Nielsen trained, again, assistants to give her chemotherapy, which slowed down cancer's progression enough so that Nielsen made it to the Antarctic spring and could be transferred to the United States for treatment — and she recovered. Years later, however, the cancer recurred. Nielsen lost the second battle and died at age 57.

A similar situation, where the only physician at a research station in Antarctica fell seriously ill, occurred in 1961. In this case, the

Russian research station physician *Vladislav Rogozov* did an appendectomy on himself with a help of a meteorologist who belonged to the station's staff. Because of these cases, the current practice is that the research stations have two physicians.

When Nielsen later wrote her experiences into a book, she emphasized how all members of the community were essential for the survival of the community. Each link in the chain is relevant and all are equal.

Naturally the role of each member is emphasized in a small community in isolation. As the size of a community increases, the importance of its members' roles gets diluted. Yet even this enormous human jigsaw is built in such a way that it is full of essential pieces, and the pieces are specialized in a variety of ways. When you turn on the water tap, someone is constantly in the background ensuring the water's quality. Several pieces of the jigsaw are also participating in the fact that the water moves at all. Quite a number of people are continuously ensuring that you have electricity. Maintenance of this humanity's jigsaw requires primary production, processing, maintenance, care, communication, training, development, commerce, logistics, protection, regulation, and so forth. If some greater link should fail, we would be in trouble.

It is odd that some jobs are considered more valuable than others when everyone is needed for the completeness. Instead, it is natural that salaries vary, since job requirements and responsibilities vary. However, the current pay spread represents the same general extremism as does thinking.

Real equality is demonstrated by the fact that everyone ends up as pieces in the very same, flat jigsaw, as parts of a common game. A brain surgeon's expertise would go completely wasted unless some had developed and prepared instruments for him; built operating theaters; and guaranteed light, heat, and cleanliness. In order for a community to have obtained a brain surgeon, a long chain of top professionals has ensured a brain surgeon's upbringing, training, nourishment supply, health care, clothing, transportation, entertainment, and so forth.

A jigsaw would be beautiful if all its pieces felt that they are in the right places. We are all unique, so we all have our own unique places as part of the same completeness. Unlike a usual jigsaw, a human jigsaw, however, is constantly changing. Thus a natural place is perhaps not as natural after five to ten years, and it's time to swap places. It is completely natural. Instead it is unnatural in the light of the ever changing and flowing nature of life to force the pieces of the jigsaw into the same positions for decades.

Because we are so unique, we are not supposed to emulate our best friend in a career choice. It is equally pointless to compare our own position to another position in a jigsaw, because that other position would abrade us even though the fit is perfect for someone else. In the end, only we ourselves know what is most suitable for us. Other people can certainly advise and give ideas, but they should not decide. Outsiders, with their inadequate knowledge, can't make decisions on another person's life. That, again, would represent a fallacy of control.

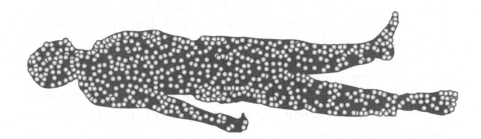

5.9 Reason and heart

In addition to a jigsaw, another metaphor, which we could use, is a giant. I am a skin cell in a giant's big toe. You are an optic nerve cell. Some celebrity is an epithelial cell in a leg's main artery. You and I, with all the other people, form a huge giant. We all are one.

Because I am the skin cell in the big toe, it would be absurd for me to be jealous of the celebrity, who is the epithelial cell in the leg's main artery. After all, that artery brings oxygen to the big toe, so I'm kept alive! I am therefore pleased that the main arteries' epithelial cells everywhere are in excellent condition. It works for my own benefit that the giant is healthy.

You can feel great pleasure of your own level of maturity if you experience the world like this: we are all one.

When enthusiasm of oneness arises, it also opens the door for naiveté. One should keep in mind, however, that only a part of humanity has advanced to such a maturity level, and you live in the prevailing reality. Therefore, everyone should still not be trusted. Complete naiveté would be possible only in a thoroughly developed world.

Thus in modifying one's world view, one should not hurtle from one extreme to another, but here, too, it is wise to follow a driving school instructor's teachings: a slight movement is often sufficient in straightening out an error. Here a subtle movement is represented by the fact that one should keep in mind various intentions and maturity levels of people.

6 From satisfaction to happiness

At this point, you have already advanced far. Distorted thinking patterns and silent assumptions are rapidly straightening out and outdated silent assumptions are getting updated. Knowing the basic human desires taught you to understand yourself somewhat better. While reading of maturation into an authentic adult, you may have even experienced an enlightenment of some degree.

In practice you should now have a one-story, unfinished house on a firm foundation. It is time to make the finishing touches on your house. Tiles need to be grouted, baseboards are missing just about everywhere and when it comes to the walls, you should decide whether to paint or to wallpaper.

Finishing touches for your house are represented by this final chapter of positive people. They are those who are already living a productive, creative, and happy life. When you seek to be prolific, creative, and happy, you should find out what are the secrets of the people who are already all that. A field of study finding out these secrets has its own name: positive psychology. Behind positivity there are, in fact, many reasons. From a large bin, I picked up those study results that have made greatest impression on me.

When it comes to people living productive, creative, and happy lives, someone usually hastens to say: "It sure is easy for those fortunate, well-off folks to smile!" Therefore, a story needs to be told why the psychologist *Mihaly Csikszentmihalyi* became interested in positive psychology. After the Second World War, he made an observation that the assertive, happy, and successful people he knew in his childhood were like empty shells after having lost everything in the war. However, there were individual adults who were serene and who had not lost their hope, life's purpose, and desire. These rare people were the ones who, in turn, cast hope to others. These select few were not the people who would have been expected to assume the role of a light- and hope-bearer because before the war they were not necessarily the most respected, successful, educated, and skilled. Thus positive psychology is something else than a pre-smoothed path and being born with a silver spoon in one's mouth. In fact, a follow-up study, which was started back in the 1950s, shows that while people's incomes have nearly tripled after the beginning of the study, human happiness has not increased. It is true that lack generates unhappiness, but research has shown also that *maximal* happiness is reachable already with a middle income.

6.1 Happiness

What, then, is human happiness? First, before definitions, it should be reminded that happiness *doesn't* mean that a person is happy every moment. Especially perfectionists may have a perception that a person has to be happy all the time and think only perfectly positive thoughts. Social psychologist *Norman M. Bradburn* has defined happiness in this way: we are happy when we have *more* positive emotions than negative. We are unhappy if the situation is other way around.

There are three types of happiness: light short-term, deeply satisfying long-term, and life purpose happiness.

Short-term happiness is "feel-good" happiness. It is that happiness that comes, for example, from getting new shoes, watching a good movie, from an excellent dinner, and a fun-filled celebration. Duration of such "feel-good" happiness is usually a few hours. However, one can learn to increase happiness further by various techniques, such as, for example, by savoring slowly, saving the best for last, or by feeling gratitude. It is typical for this "feel-good" happiness that rewards get smaller over time. It means that a happiness-generating experience has to be larger, deeper, more earth-shattering, more beautiful or more touching in the subsequent times in order to generate the same amount of short-term happiness as in the first time. For example, if an amusement park's roller coaster seemed simply wild during the first few times, at some point it feels far too tame. In order to obtain the same feeling, one should get a fiercer ride, more sheer drops, more upright climbs, steeper bends, and the entire tour should last a lot longer.

If a person's perception of happiness is that it is purely and simply "feel-good" happiness, he is constantly looking for experiences that generate them. Let's assume that money was no obstacle. Then a person could live in a "feel-good" hunt constantly. After a vacation and partying, one could plan the next vacation and partying. Sounds great, but this kind of person would not feel completely happy. After some time, life would feel empty and superficial.

A seeker of short-term happiness is called *a hedonist*. Hedonism can be further divided into two different types of practicing hedonism: self-indulgence and self-denial. Self-indulgence as a source for short-term happiness everyone understands. It is that constant partying, vacationing, shopping, sex, and perhaps narcotic substances. As rewards grow smaller over time, stakes need to be increased. That second type of hedonism, self-denial, sounds probably surprising to many people in this context. In self-denial the pleasure comes from *avoidance* of discomfort and stress. If you don't fall in love, you won't get abandoned. If you don't drink, you won't get hangovers. If you don't eat too much, you won't suffer from indigestion. If you don't travel, you won't be placed at risk. If you don't invest in an expensive gadget or vehicle, you don't need to worry about it being stolen. If you don't strive for anything, you won't fail. If you avoid succeeding, you don't end up being envied.

A slogan for a short-term happiness seeker is that a person should live in the moment. It is true that we should live here and now instead of constantly looking back in the past or be at least a couple of steps in the future. However, being in this moment has different depth options. One can hover in constant emptiness and superficiality here and now, or one can be anchored to a deeper level of happiness here and now.

While the "feel-good" happiness thrills only for a few hours, long-lasting happiness keeps happy for years and decades. Furthermore, there is no need to worry about decreasing premiums. Long-lasting happiness is also known as value-based happiness. Those who enjoy long-lasting happiness don't need constant pleasant sensations. There is no need for a cheek-burning, continuous fire at a fireplace when life has a deeper purpose that keeps the coals of happiness constantly alive. When a person experiences such happiness, he also notices more easily the little joys of everyday life. Value-based happiness is in that way odd happiness that sometimes it also brings unpleasant sensations. For example, one is subjected to a degree of discomfort when one has to make sacrifices for one's own happiness. An example of this is people who hope to have children of their own. They know that raising children is not always going to be mere sunshine. Another example is an amount of work people are willing to invest in order to achieve their dreams. For some it means reading thousands of pages, for others more than ten thousand hours of practice in controlling an instrument. Gardening, handicraft, baking, construction work — all of them have elements of long-lasting happiness. They require study and work, development through practice, and enjoyment of the end results.

Psychologist Mihaly Csikszentmihalyi has studied a phenomenon closely related to long-term happiness, which is called *flow*. It is when someone is so absorbed in doing something that he doesn't even notice how time goes by. The flow state is also called an optimal experience or "the zone." People who access the flow state describe that in a way they themselves cease to exist. That is when neither hunger nor fatigue is troubling, and all other things apart from the current interest and focus are far from one's mind. In the flow state, a person is in a state of reality that deviates from a normal everyday life.

It is not necessary to "do" something in order to get to the flow state. Flow can arise even when one is sitting in the seat of a viewer or a listener and when a performance, film, TV program, game, lecture, or discussion is fully absorbing. However, it is not a question of mere passive monitoring and being entertained. In order for a viewer to achieve flow, he has to be strongly activated at the level of his mind, be really interested, become aware of something, rise above the everyday life and feel involved at some level.

When one, himself, is a doer or maker, then getting into flow is fostered by a high level of a skill or a craftsmanship. An aspiring graphic designer, seamstress, snowboarder, researcher, carpenter, builder, cook, baker, gardener, painter, composer, writer, musician, capoeira-dancer, traceur, and so forth does not necessarily access easily and all that often the flow state when he is still learning his field. As one develops in his field, flow increases. It has been observed that after practicing around ten years a profession or a hobby, a leap occurs to real mastery when we talk about a field that requires high technical expertise or training. There still has to remain some challenge, however, because excess comfort and habituation take away from the flow state.

In a state of flow, a person reaches his very best. Therefore, the traditional advice for a perfectionist to reduce his performance level doesn't sound right. Everyone, also a perfectionist, has to have a chance to reach his full potential. Everyone, also a perfectionist, should still prioritize his tasks and save the sharpest energy for one's greatest passions. Because the fact is that a person has to have passion for the thing that absorbs him into the state of flow.

Apathy or the state of indifference is opposite from the state of flow. In apathy, nothing interests and time drags. Thus there is time to think of one's fatigue, thirst, hunger, feelings of misery, and bleakness of the whole world. Apathy is often associated with depression, and depression is *always* associated with distorted thought patterns and outdated silent assumptions. Apathy could well be envisaged as a labyrinth in which it is nearly impossible to access the flow state center, because all of the time is spent in distortion deadlocks. Isn't this yet another good reason why it is worthwhile investing time in straightening thoughts and updating silent assumptions?

A life purpose is associated with long-term happiness, even though some researchers, such as psychologist *Martin Seligman,* separate life purpose yet into its distinct section of happiness. People, who are satisfied with their lives, have all three types of happiness — short-term happiness, long-term happiness, and a purpose for life. Most satisfied are those who emphasize long-term happiness and a life purpose.

A life purpose is defined in such a way that people use their talents and strengths in service of a larger idea. A meaningful life in a service of mankind — or the entire planet — is a *doubly* happy life in a sense that both a recipient and a donor get happy. A donor gets a sense of life purpose from his service and also a feeling of being part of something bigger. A recipient gets concrete help, which he needs in order to move forward and, at some point, to progress into a position of a donor, where he, in turn, can pay it forward.

The research has surprisingly shown that the first ingredient of happiness, that is, short-term happiness has, after all, a very small share in life satisfaction people experience. It is really just a spice, that cinnamon on top of rice pudding. The second ingredient of happiness, long-lasting happiness, is very important. It is that rice pudding itself. The most important factor in the studies was, however, the third ingredient, that finding of one's life purpose through servicing others. That third ingredient is Christmas when that rice pudding is eaten (in at least some Nordic countries, mind you).

However, all three species of happiness have their own important significance, even though their emphases differ. During Christmas, it would be annoying over a cup of rice pudding if cinnamon was forgotten in a store. If Christmas was taken away, that rice pudding wouldn't taste as good. Licking mere cinnamon during Christmas doesn't warm anyone's heart.

What could be concluded if these three elements of happiness were examined against the social maturity described in the previous chapter? As you remember, with social maturation the human perspective expands and expands and even after that it still expands. At the same time, a human being has his boundaries of control in check, and there is no fallacy. A socially mature person has first budded from the pudding into a grain of sand and understands, watching from still farther off distance, that as a grain of sand he is part of a vast sandy desert. Therefore, it is important to take care of the welfare of the whole sandy desert; its purity, it not dripping into earth's bosom or not flying into the winds of heaven in a storm, and not only focus on coping as a single grain of sand.

Because a socially mature person sees the world differently — in a way that one single large is comprised of all the tiny fragments — the third component of happiness, a purpose in life, is easy for him to reach. At the lower levels of maturity, others than "myself" are not either even of interest or one is interested in the welfare of others for hypocritical reasons, such as, for example, because a perfect person *is supposed to be* interested in the wholeness or because even that may be of somehow beneficial first and foremost to "myself."

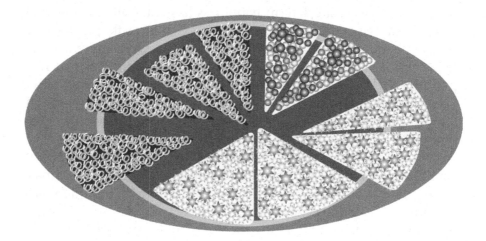

According to Martin Seligman, two slices of the happiness pie are short-term happiness, about three or four slices are long-term happiness, and five or four slices are life purpose-based happiness. Therefore, at a low social maturation level, one may be deprived of about half of the happiness pie. What could be a better advertisement for social maturation than an opportunity to gain access to an entire happiness pie?

Again, by what means was a higher social maturity level achievable? You already know how to answer: by developing a capacity for empathy, by eliminating the fallacy of control, and by bearing a right size of responsibility. Can you think of what is even a greater prerequisite for your social maturation than the above-mentioned three factors? That is high self-worth. Feeling worthy is the necessary ingredient for your social maturation. You are worthy for a fact, but you also have to believe in it yourself. What then is a prerequisite for self-worth? It is love. You have to love yourself in order to feel worthy. If you don't love yourself yet, learn to tell yourself gently and frequently that you love you. Both loving one's self and the capacity for empathy can be fully learned, and they only need to be practiced.

As was stated in the beginning of this subchapter, happiness is having *more* positive emotions than negative. Therefore, negative experiences and feelings are to be expected, and everyone gets to enjoy them. It is possible, however, to round off the edges of adversities with a right attitude. Edges of adversities become rounded with social maturation.

Often a misfortune has a chance built into it. It would be good if you would eventually get to say: "It was a blessing in disguise!" That phrase may be used when an accident or misfortune was not as bad as it could have been, but it can also be used when an accident or misfortune, either directly or indirectly, brings something new and great into life. There is a law of nature that a vacuum gets filled. You yourself can affect how that vacuum gets filled.

6.2 Six strengths and virtues of positive people

Research has shown that a positive person has six personality strengths and virtues, which are universal.
1. **Wisdom and knowledge**
2. **Courage**
3. **Humanity**
4. **Justice**
5. **Temperance**
6. **Transcendence**

Wisdom and knowledge is a virtue and strength of a positive person. It is an indication of human creativity, a desire for knowledge, a willingness to learn, openness, an ability to see things in their right proportions, and to have a broad perspective on issues. A creative person is capable of, among other things, inventing alternative ways in accomplishing things. A desire for knowledge, for example, is having interest and curiosity about topics and events currently taking place. A willingness to learn is a desire to learn new skills, knowledge, and larger thematic entities. A willingness to learn includes also the ability for critical thinking and discernment. Openness refers to an ability to examine issues from different angles. Since a positive person has different perspectives on things, and he is able to see things in their right proportions, his friends and close ones often turn to him and seek advice in turning points of their own lives.

Courage is a virtue and strength of a positive person. Courage is a will and perseverance when internal or external forces try to prevent from reaching a goal. Courage means authenticity, reliability, and speaking the truth. A courageous person doesn't shrink in front of a threat, challenge, difficulty, or suffering. A courageous person ends what he has started, that is, he is capable of carrying out also long-term projects. A courageous person has enthusiasm and energy.

Humanity is a virtue and strength of a positive person. A human person takes care of others and shows kindness towards others. He does favors and good deeds for others. He has the ability to love and be loved. He reflects social intelligence, which means that he recognizes his and other people's motives and feelings.

Justice is a virtue and strength of a positive person. Justice is social awareness, a desire to be a member in a healthy community. A fair person wants to treat everyone equally and openly. Besides fairness, a sense of justice includes leadership and cooperation. A fair person organizes group activities and sees that they also get realized. A fair person works well as a member of a group.

Temperance is a virtue and strength of a positive person. Temperance is a strength, which protects from excessiveness, exaggerations, misuse, misconduct, and abuse. Temperance is humility, deliberation, and self-regulation. A positive person, whose strength is temperance, is able to forgive. He lets the results speak for themselves. As a deliberate person, he is careful in making his choices, and he doesn't hasten to say something he would regret later. Self-regulation enables him to regulate his feelings and actions.

Transcendence is a virtue and strength of a positive person. Transcendence means going beyond the limits of an ordinary experience and being better or greater than what is considered typical. Transcendence is appreciation of arts and beauty, gratitude, hope, and humor. It is also religiousness or spirituality. A transcendent person notices the beauty found in all sectors of life. He also notices the admirable skill and know-how of other people. He is aware of and grateful for the good things and events in his life. He has hope, that is, he expects the best and works diligently to achieve it. He likes to laugh, may tease good-naturedly, and brings smiles to people's faces. He has a higher purpose in life.

Emphases of these virtues and strengths vary in different groups of people. For example, courage is more powerful in young positive people and transcendence, in turn, among older positive people. "Virtues and strengths of a heart," that is, zest for life, gratitude, hope, and love affect more in people's life satisfaction than the "virtues and strengths of a brain," such as a desire for knowledge and a willingness to learn. An interesting detail in the studies is that self-regulation of parents, which is part of temperance, linked more strongly to their children's life satisfaction than that of their own. That result confirms other study results, which claim the home's chaos, unpredictability, and unfairness in behavior and actions are harmful to a child's development.

The strengths and virtues of a positive human form a very limited set — only a set of six —, but still it includes temperance as its own entirety and therefore it is considered important. Temperance is the opposite of extreme thinking and extreme deeds. Temperance is the golden mean. Temperance resides in the middle of a seesaw. In temperance, a seesaw is level, it neither sways nor falls. A seesaw, which is askew, has instead its other end against the gravel.

In this book, there has been alongside an idea of different segments, and how the extreme ends of these segments represent almost always imbalance, and how the middle region of a segment is the goal worthwhile pursuing. Temperance expresses this directly, but also other human strengths and virtues represent a middle region of a segment. For example, courage refers to a middle region of a courage segment. On one extreme of a courage segment, one would have cowardice, on the other, recklessness. It has to be separately mentioned about courage that it is rarely an inborn quality. Courage is an attainable skill. For example, a confident adult performer of large stages may have been a blushing child whom the teacher asked repeatedly to speak louder. Courage grows step-by-step when one acts in spite of one's fears.

When you look at all the six strengths and virtues of a positive, happy person, what degree of social maturity do you think they represent?

6.3 Choice

You may be using expressions of this sort in your talk: "Then I had to ..." "It happened to me that ..." "I ended up accidentally..." If you are in a wise company, the person you are talking to corrects you calmly that you yourself made all those choices. You dispute that you would have ended to certain situations through your own choice. The person you are talking to repeats with a smile: "You made all those choices, there were always other options."

You have to admit your responsibility: you have made all by yourself a lot of choices over the long term, the consequences of which appear later. It is not a question of some kind of drifting, fate, or luck, the question is of a long series of choices.

We start every day by making choices the minute we wake up. It is our own choice whether we brush our teeth at all, whether we brush them superficially or properly. Very soon our choices turn into a routine. If our choice is to go without brushing our teeth from day-to-day, and if as a result of that choice we get heart disease during middle age that begun from an infection in the mouth, then the choice was entirely ours. Then we can't say that our *fate* was hard when it took us to the brink of the grave at fifty years of age.

People face, of course, things that are outside of their own choices, but their share is certainly much less than the people themselves think and argue. Responsibility for the turning points in our lives is easier to pass outside of ourselves. M. Scott Peck is right: we all have at least some personality disorder and thus we avoid taking responsibility.

Why is it worthwhile getting rid of that responsibility-shunning personality disorder for the most part? First of all, a person's self-worth and self-confidence increase from a realization that he is much more, and more often at the controls than he has dared to think. Once one eventually believes in this truth, he is a better one's own life's researcher and a maker of changes. A one's own life's researcher stops to make observations: "I chose option A, so that's why now, ten years later, I'm at a point B. I no longer want to be at a point B, so what choices should I make now, so I could get to a point C?"

When a person makes choices between different options in his life, he tries to choose the best or most appealing choice at that moment — assuming that his self-worth is sufficient. In his choices, a person emphasizes those options that are closest to his strongest desires. When you take responsibility that you yourself made your own choices, at the same time, you learn more about yourself and your values. The more you learn about yourself, the better you can become your authentic self.

6.4 Authentic adulthood

A high degree of social maturity means being an authentic adult. An authentic adult appreciates himself and others. An authentic adult works for everyone's benefits, recognizes his boundaries of control, and consciously avoids falling into a trap of distortions. An authentic adult bears responsibility of a correct size — not too much, not too little. You have also already concluded that an authentic adult seeks balance and moves towards the center region of a seesaw. This kind of seeking balance is also an ability to give up endlessly having fun or alternatively toiling too hard. Balancing is also an ability to control one's anger. Furthermore, balancing is an ability to choose the battles, which to take part in. Each life's battle doesn't require taking part in or it is not even worthwhile taking part in, instead sometimes it is wise to walk away or even hand over the victory to another. Sometimes achieving balance requires giving up habits and outdated silent assumptions. The fact that one agrees to balancing is a sign of an authentic adulthood.

Authentic adulthood requires also perseverance. It means long-term thinking and actions, presence of mind, and toughness. Then one is capable of carrying out long-lasting projects. A perseverant person does not give up on the first setback. It, too, is perseverance that one is able to see long-term consequences of one's choices and actions.

Authentic adulthood requires also patience. Patience has much of the same as perseverance. That, too, includes presence of mind

— an ability to stay calm and efficient. Patience is more linked to one's behavior, whereas perseverance is linked more in planning and taking action. A patient person bears to wait and stay calm for a longer time compared to an impatient person who loses his temper easily and gets angry. A patient, perseverant person is also capable of putting off satisfaction and rewards to a later date. It is called delaying gratification. Thus he has an access to all ten slices of a happiness pie, for especially long-term happiness and happiness containing a purpose of life don't usually provide instant gratification. A person who is *not* able to put off satisfaction and rewards to a later date gets to enjoy only of the two slices of a happiness pie, that is, short-term happiness.

Authentic adulthood requires also an order. An order refers to both an order of the mind and an external order. When confronted with a problem, a person of an order has patience to stop and analyze and, if need be, be slow. He doesn't panic and throw a tantrum, and he doesn't destroy more. Reflection leads to different solution options, to the selection of the final solution, and its implementation. Even if the solution requires a number of attempts, the basic formula remains the same: options, selection, and implementation. With this formula, a big portion of life's problems get solved.

An external order is cleanliness and tidiness. If your creativity requires an external *dis*order, continue in your old manner. If your creativity requires an external order, carry on as before. We are all different, as you already know. Sometimes, however, external disorder and hoarding form a barrier for life. A large amount of material things can grow into a heavy anchor, which ties into one place. Then decisions are determined by material things, not on the basis of one's own desires and needs. Ask yourself: what kind of role does an external order or the lack thereof have in my life? Do material things make decisions on my behalf? Which of the two is serving whom?

Authentic adulthood requires also dedication to truth. In other words, an authentic adult is honest. Dedication to truth was already included in a positive person's strengths and virtues. It was mentioned in connection with *Courage*, since sometimes honesty requires courage. It is easier to lie even to oneself, for instance, by accusing others of one's own problems, instead of admitting one's own involvement and bear the responsibility. Although lying to oneself and others may save from a momentary pain, dishonesty in the background is often left to grow into a big pain. It would be easier to stick to the truth and in a matter-of-fact way deal with the sufferings of everyday life and take them one by one off the agenda.

Companies and organizations are sometimes compared to humans. It is said that a large company or an organization is like a human being with a low intelligent quotient (IQ). This refers to the fact that when some obscurity appears, a client finds from a company or organization no one who understands the matter and who would be able to solve the problems. The matter is only transferred from one employee to another and time passes. The personnel may be polite on the surface towards the client, but at the same time indifferent towards the matter needing resolving. This could equally well be described as a large company or organization having a low degree of social maturity. When a problem arises no one takes responsibility, but carries out only one's own familiar, narrow work obligation he is paid for to do. This type of company or organization is a child, not an authentic adult. Intelligence and maturity is not one and the same, and thus also a high-tech company can be just as much of a child as any other company or organization.

Are you working in a child company or a child organization? Does the company or organization have a capacity for empathy? If the capacity for empathy is found, then the aim of the company or organization is to improve in some way all of our lives instead of striving only for its own benefit. Does the company or organization go into extremes in expectations, decision-making, practices, and behavior? Are the boundaries of control pudding-like or intact? Are the pudding-like boundaries shrunk so that the company or organization struggles beneath the yoke of the owners or financiers? Are the pudding-like boundaries expanded so that the company or organization attempts to mold their employees and manage their free personal lives and spare time? Does your workplace seek balance?

Does your company or employer make long-term plans, work long-term, and is it patient? A company, which in its lust for quick profits drives people to plight or danger or pollutes the environment, is not perseverant. Unfortunately, damages done by immature companies can be massive in size compared to the consequences of whims of human children.

Is the operation of the company or organization honest and open? Which prevails at the workplace, fear or trust? Is there an order? Is the company or organization able to, and does it dare to, accept criticism? Does it bear responsibility? Does the company or organization pigeonhole employees as parts of a machine, as filers of the one and the same thing? Does it allow corporate psychopaths or narcissists to make havoc at the workplace? Is the company or organization preserving this planet for the future generations? How do you, with your own share, contribute to a continuous maturation of your workplace?

6.4 Main ingredient

Love is the most important, most durable, most flexible, and most persevering thread in a yarn of life. Love can be defined in many ways. One of the most successful definitions is this: Love is a will to extend, stretch up, and straighten out in such a way that it supports both one's own and other people's growth. This growth refers in particular to maturation into an authentic adult.

In human growth, adversities constitute their own share of an upwards climb, like horizontal rungs of a ladder. Hence, on the basis of this definition, it is *not* love when parents make every effort to protect a child from hardships. From the perspective of love, too much protection and leveling the road for another one is the same thing as sawing off the rungs of a ladder so that the other one can't climb upwards, towards his most authentic self. Hence too much protection and leveling of the road means holding a person unchanged, immature, undeveloped, and easily controllable. In the same way, the horizontal rungs of the ladder are missing from a child whose parents are shaping their child according to their own preferences. For these parents, a child is not here as a loan — like a child in this life is supposed to be — but they consider their child as part of their property, and in their own opinion, they can do with their property as they wish. Based on what you have already read, you know that these parents suffer from a fallacy of control. These parents have not yet socially matured, but they may still mature. They, too, can mature until the last breath they take.

The most valuable, most precious, most beautiful, and the greatest act of love parents can ever give to their child is to accept the child as he is. When parents give this gift, a child gets healthy self-worth. If, instead, the parents' perception is that their mission is to customize their child to their own liking, a child doesn't get this gift of acceptance. Such a child may use the rest of his life seeking for approval, his self-worth is low, and he often suffers from depression.

When parents themselves have their silent assumption of approval in a healthy range, their child's desire to become independent is not threatening to them. Then it is possible for the child to become both independent and his own authentic self.

Those parents who swear by the name of discipline are actually engaging in undisciplined discipline. This designation comes from Scott M. Peck. Undisciplined discipline is slapping, screaming, silent treatment, sneering, spitefulness, taking vengeance, and belittling. Undisciplined discipline is completely meaningless and unproductive. A child of undisciplined discipline doesn't develop an ability to delay satisfaction and rewards later, and an authentic adulthood realizes only later in life or it doesn't realize at all.

Above undisciplined discipline there is love. In other words: even in a home of chaos and undisciplined discipline, a child may grow up to be an authentic adult, if there has been love in that home. Similarly, from a family, where the parents themselves have had perseverance, patience, and an order, but the home has been without love, children may grow up unruly, disorganized, and problematic.

Parents are forgiven for a lot of mistakes, if love is recognizable behind everything. However, one unforgivable mistake has to be mentioned separately — in a name discipline, one should *never* threaten a child with abandonment. It is possible that at the same time one deprives a child of a sense of security for the rest of his life.

One expression of love is time. Love takes time. If parents settle love with mere professions of love, which are in no relation with their *acts*, a child finally recognizes the difference between empty professions and genuine caring.

Love is caring. Love is recognizing needs. Love is everyday life. Love is safety, order, and habits. Love is teaching basic life skills. Love is listening, answering to questions, discussing, advising, and story-telling. Love explains and rationalizes. Love is stroking one's hair, hugging, embracing, and patting encouragingly on a shoulder. Love is humor. Love sets limits. Love is relaxing in one thing, tightening in another. Love is temperance. Love is honesty. Love is recognition of one's own ignorance and searching for answers together. Love is patience. Love is suffering alongside. Love is appreciation. Love is respect. Love allows a human being to become his authentic self. Love is another's perspective. Love is apologizing and forgiveness. Love is gratitude and saying thank you. Love is keeping hope alive.

It is said that only gardening is important and even that is not very important. It would, instead, be justifiable to say that only rearing and loving children is important and that indeed is important. Child-rearing is by far the most important and valuable work in this world. Nothing exceeds that. Every Nobel Prize won is like "playing in a sandbox" compared to child rearing. The prevailing systems in the world should recognize this fact and give a better chance for carrying out this honorable work. Carrying out this work with dignity requires time from the entire village. Even a cold money-man is capable of understanding that investment of love into childhood is an invest-ment worth money for a society, even if he in his narrow-mindedness wouldn't think for a second the humane losses, which always exceed money in importance.

High quality child-rearing is important for all possible imaginable reasons. The fact is that a foundation of a child's mental health is cast in childhood. A child, who is loved and who is taken care of, feels he is valuable. A child, who has high self-worth, sees this world completely differently than the one who feels unworthy. For a child who has high self-worth, life's inevitable setbacks are opportunities to grow. A child, who has high self-worth, solves the problems of our planet in due course. Even a cold money-man has to acknowledge that such a child is the most important asset of the world. What could possibly go ahead of it?

Noticeable in the definition of love is also the fact that it covers *one self and others*. Thus it is not love that one neglects himself and only focuses on servicing others. So does a martyr. His service doesn't rise from love, but from the feelings of worthlessness or from the pursuit of perfection. The pursuit of perfection is worthwhile mentioning as its own, because some people serve other people only because they assume that that is how a perfect person acts. True love means neither that a person works for his own growth, forgetting others. True love is a will that growth takes place for *everyone* and a loving person carries out this will according to his capabilities. Love, indeed, is a will, not only a desire. A will includes also acts in addition to a desire.

If maturing into an authentic adult has stopped for some reason, it is possible to continue on one's own. Maturation, unlike growth in height, continues always, if one invests time and thought in it.

Compilation of this book and the synthesis of new data was my act of love for you, me, and us. Your charming and beautiful house is now beginning to be ready for a move-in. It will still take some time, however, to get it all decorated comfortably. The yard is still without any plans and implementation, but you already know how to continue with this on your own. You still have work to do, but it is wonderful, loving work. You are not doing this work only for your own sake, but for all of us. Warmest thanks are due to you.

References

Aristotle. 1962. The Nicomachean ethics. Indianapolis: Bobbs-Merrill.

Aron, Elaine N. 2013. Erityisherkkä ihminen. Helsinki: Nemo. [Aron, Elaine N. 1999. The highly sensitive person: how to thrive when the world overwhelms you. New York: HarperCollins Publishers.]

Babiak, Paul & Hare, Robert D. 2007. Snakes in suits: when psychopaths go to work. New York: HaperCollins Publishers.

Beck, Aaron T. 1976. Cognitive therapies and emotional disorders. New York: New American Library.

Beck, Aaron T., Brown, Gary, Steer, Robert A. & Weissman, Arlene N. 1991. Factor analysis of the dysfunctional attitude scale in a clinical population. Psychological assessment: A Journal of Consulting and Clinical Psychology, vol. 3(3), 478–483.

Boyes, Alice. 2013. 50 Common cognitive distortions. A giant list of ubiquitous cognitive distortions. Referred to on 7.7.2015. http://bit.ly/1MpFtvi

Bradburn, Norman M. 1969. The structure of psychological well-being. Chicago: Aldine Publishing Company.

Breathnach, Sarah Ban. 1995. Simple abundance: a daybook of comfort and joy. New York: Warner Books.

Burns, David D. 1999. Feeling good – the new mood therapy. New York: HarperCollins Publishers.

Burns, David. 2014. Feeling good. Referred to on 10.4.2015. TEDx Talks. http://bit.ly/1Pdo9NV

Cognitive distortion. Wikipedia. Referred to on 7.7.2015. http://bit.ly/1O17E4b

Csikszentmihalyi, Mihaly. 2004. Flow, the secret of happiness. Referred to on 7.15.2015. http://bit.ly/1HMmOpy

Diamandis, Peter H. & Kotler, Steven. 2012. Abundance. The future is better than you think. New York: Free Press.

Dienstmann, Giovanni. Types of meditation – an overview of 23 meditation techniques. Live and dare. Meditation blog and non-sectarian spirituality. Referred to on 9.7.2015. http://bit.ly/1EQU5kQ

Eres, Robert, Decety, Jean, Louis, Winnifred R. & Molenbergs, Pascal. 2015. Individual differences in local gray matter density are associated with differences in affective and cognitive empathy. NeuroImage, vol. 117, 305–310.

GoodTherapy.org staff. 2015. 20 Cognitive distortions and how they affect your life. Referred to on 7.7.2015. http://bit.ly/1Hqg57o

Grohol, John M. 15 Common cognitive distortions. Referred to 7.7.2105. http://bit.ly/1TxCaGG

Hagelin, John. 2009. A scientific introduction to transcendental meditation by Dr. John Hagelin. Referred to on 6.6.2015. http://bit.ly/1fCYTms

Jandai, Jon. 2011. Life is easy. Why do we make it so hard? Referred to on 9.23.2015. TEDx Talks. http://bit.ly/1iydnBh

Jeffries, Susan. 1988. Feel the fear and do it anyway. New York & Toronto: Random House.

Kegan, Robert. 1982. The evolving self: problem and process in human development. Cambridge, Massachusetts: Harvard University Press.

Kegan, Robert. 1994. In over our heads: the mental demands of modern life. Cambridge, Massachusetts: Harvard University Press.

Malkin, Craig. 2015. Rethinking narcissism: the bad – and surprising good – about feeling special. New York: HarperCollins Publishers.

Manninen, Mari. 2015. Lapsivuode Kiinassa: Ei suihkua kuukauteen, mummo pitää jöötä. Isovanhemmat hoitavat lastenlapset ja aikuiset lapset vanhat vanhempansa. Referred to on 6.7.2015. http://bit.ly/1GhBgob

Niagara Falls Facts. Referred to on 6.24.2015. http://bit.ly/1eWIwjG

Nielsen, Jerri & Vollers, Maryanne. 2001. Ice Bound: A doctor's incredible battle for survival at the South Pole. New York: Hyperion.

Peck, M. Scott. 1978. The road less travelled. A new psychology of love, traditional values and spiritual growth. Lontoo: Rider.

Reiss, Steven. 2000. Who am I? The 16 basic desires that motivate our actions and define our personalities. New York: Jeremy P. Tarcher / Putnam – a member of Penguin Putnam Inc.

Roth, Bob. 2014. Transcendental meditation technique - a complete introduction. Referred to on 6.6.2015. http://bit.ly/1uhn67V

Seligman, Martin E. P. 2004.The New Era of Positive Psychology. Referred to on 7.15.2015. http://bit.ly/1sYaSNc

Seligman, Martin E. P. & Csikszentmihalyi, Mihaly. 2000. Positive psychology. An introduction. American Psychologist vol. 55, 5-14.

Seligman, Martin E. P., Steen Tracy A., Park, Nansook & Peterson, Christopher. 2005. Positive psychology progress. Empirical validation of interventions. American Psychologist vol. 60, 410-421.

Smith, Richard H. & Kim, Sung Hee. 2007. Comprehending envy. Psychological Bulletin. Vol. 133, 46–64.

Stoeber, Joachim. 2014. How other-oriented perfectionism differs from self-oriented and socially prescribed perfectionism. Journal of Psychopathology and Behavioral Assessment, vol. 36, 329–338.

Suomalaisen Lääkäriseuran Duodecimin ja Suomen Psykiatriyhdistys ry:n asettama työryhmä. 2014. Käypä hoito. Depressio. Referred to on 6.7.2015. http://bit.ly/1RukLRE

Telkänranta, Helena. 2015. Millaista on olla eläin? Helsinki: Suomalaisen Kirjallisuuden Seura.

Thurston, Mark & Fazel, Christopher. 1992. The Edgar Cayce handbook for creating your future. Toronto: Random House.

Tolle, Eckhart. 1999. Practicing the power of now: essential teachings, meditations, and exercises from the power of now. Novato, Kalifornia: New World Library.

Tolle, Eckhart. 2005. A new earth: awakening to your life's purpose. New York: Penguin Group.

Vilkuna, Kustaa. 1997. Vuotuinen ajantieto. Helsinki: Otava.

Ware, Bronnie. 2012. The top five regrets of the dying. A life transformed by the dearly departing. Worldwide: Hay House.

Lightning Source UK Ltd.
Milton Keynes UK
UKOW05f1120091216

289573UK00014B/217/P